ANDY'S BRAVO SCRAPBOOK

Twenty Years Behind the Scenes *of the*
REAL HOUSEWIVES *and the* BRAVOVERSE

Andy Cohen

ANDY'S Bravo SCRAPBOOK

Andy Cohen Books
CROWN
NEW YORK

An Andy Cohen Book
Published by Crown
An imprint of the Crown Publishing Group
A division of Penguin Random House LLC
1745 Broadway
New York, NY 10019
crownpublishing.com
penguinrandomhouse.com

Library of Congress Cataloging-in-Publication Data is available upon request.

Hardcover ISBN 979-8-217-09014-3
Signed edition ISBN: 979-8-217-39929-1
Target edition ISBN: 979-8-217-39944-4
Ebook ISBN 979-8-217-09019-8

Editors: Gillian Blake and Lori Kusatzky
Editorial assistant: Jessica Jean Scott
Production editor: Abby Oladipo
Cover and interior designer: Laura Palese
Production: Jessica Heim
Copy editor: Ruth Anne Phillips
Proofreaders: Nicole Ramirez, Robin Slutzky, and Sarah Rutledge
Compositors: Nick Patton and Hannah Hunt
Publicist: Mary Moates and Lindsay Cook
Marketer: Julie Cepler

Manufactured in China

10 9 8 7 6 5 4 3 2 1

First Edition

The authorized representative in the EU for product safety and compliance is Penguin Random House Ireland, Morrison Chambers, 32 Nassau Street, Dublin D02 YH68, Ireland, https://eu-contact.penguin.ie.

THIS BOOK IS DEDICATED TO EACH AND EVERY REAL HOUSEWIFE AND BRAVOLEBRITY. WHAT A LONG, STRANGE TRIP IT'S BEEN!

SILENCE=DEATH

WHEN I look back at the epic adventure that has been my twenty-plus years at Bravo, my memories are filled with love and fun and a lot of drama. I'm lucky I've been taking personal photos from the start because they capture so well the magical time I've had with these incredible people, with whom I share incredible affinity and friendship. Many of the pics are also really funny and iconic, some with combinations of people who today would not even share the same *room* with one another, much less the same photograph! And it's amazing to me, especially as I look back at the older pictures, not only how far we've all come, but how much we've remained the same. We all came up on this ride together. Bravo made us all famous.

The backbone of this book is an incredible series of behind-the-scenes photos I've taken, mainly at reunion shows. As you know from watching, I'm seated in the middle, with housewives and Bravolebrities flanking me. It was about a year into doing reunions when I started to grab my camera, a digital at first and then an iPhone, and snap some quick pictures from my vantage point, to the left and to the right.

The reunion photos say so much. You can see the nerves on the women's faces. You can see anticipation, optimism, perfect glam, a little fear . . . and maybe a little hunger, too. Had I taken the pics at the end of the day, they might convey something a little different (predominantly exhaustion and relief). As the reunion shows themselves have become such a part of pop culture and meme history, these photographs most likely correlate with your own memories of iconic moments from each episode. I think of these photos as great examples of pop art. Some of the women don't look their best; some do. But they are as real as the shows they star in.

Mixed throughout the reunion photos are other snapshots I've taken. These range from Bravo promotional events to non-*Housewives* reunions to backstage at *Watch What Happens Live*. I have pictures of my real family with my Bravo family, and of my epic *Housewives* baby shower. These photos bring up so many hilarious memories; I tried to share as many as I could (at least as many as won't piss anybody off).

As far as what hasn't stayed the same, as you look through the photos, you'll see that not only does the quality of the photographs improve but so does the quality of the women's hair, makeup, and clothes! In some of the earlier reunion photos, the women wore simple looks that they may have sported to lunch with girlfriends. But fairly early on, you start to see everything from elevated prom to Met Gala looks. At first, it was a fashion free-for-all. But after a few years we started assigning the women themes; be it colors (I've seen every variation of jewel tone known to man!) or dresses that would complement a vacation they went on. It took a minute for the women to get their heads around the idea that these dresses also need to look great when they're sitting down.

There's a difference between how one looks in a standing photo or in front of a mirror versus in a chair or couch for ten hours—often a lesson not learned until the day of the event. (The award for housewife with the most pre-show dress calamities goes to OC's Shannon Storms Beador, who has faced everything from dresses not showing up or not fitting to otherwise malfunctioning. It's been a journey!) As for my clothes (who cares, right?), I match my suit and tie with the women's colors and consider what will look good with the background of the set. My hair gets longer, shorter, longer again, and progressively grayer (then WHITE!) as the years have progressed—and you see my weight fluctuate on a twenty-pound sliding scale.

Housewives reunions have become a staple of the Bravoverse and, I'm proud to say, they've become the template for reality television in general. *We did that!* We didn't always end a season with a reunion, but as our shows became hits, reunions and "unseen footage" episodes were great solutions to extending seasons. The pictures here also give you a headline for each season, as the housewives closest to me on either side were in the reunion hot seat. We agonize over the seating charts before we film, putting the two cast members with the most drama that season immediately to my left and right. Over the years, the seating charts have become important enough to the fans that Bravo's social team releases them on reunion filming day.

Beverly
Hills

WHEN I think of the *Beverly Hills* reunions, a few things come to mind. The first is that these housewives are the most consistently well-dressed in the *Housewives* galaxy. You don't see a ton of fashion faux pas when you look through the years of *Beverly Hills*. The second is that Kyle and I have shared a lot of laughs, often finding ourselves quietly giggling, usually at some of the absurdities of our conversations (a returned bunny wrapped in cellophane!; living on a "main road"!).

Beverly Hills is the only city where two housewives have quit the show by virtue of not showing up at reunions. When Adrienne Maloof didn't turn up in season three, I was bummed because I'd always rooted for her. Looking back, I think I was more callous (too flippant) than I should have been on air about her not being there. I just wished she'd come!

ISO 100
ISO 100
ISO 100 1
ISO 100 2

ISO 100
ISO 100

ISO 100
ISO 100

I was also really disappointed when Lisa Vanderpump did not show up for the season nine reunion. At the time, I thought if she had come, we would have been able to work out the trouble between her and Kyle. The mark of a great housewife—and they both are top-tier—is being able to find middle ground in friendship that allows you to move forward. I had this vision that maybe they could figure it out in the chairs. Now, obviously, that doesn't seem within the realm of possibility, but it certainly felt within reach at the time.

It's interesting to look back on those two no-shows, because when Adrienne skipped the taping, Lisa very vocally said, "I think she wanted to stay, and she should have come, cleared up the mess, and moved on." As it turned out, Lisa was predicting her own future on the show in a way.

“ROLL TO THE LEFT AND PAT THE TOP. ROLL AND PAT.” —ERIKA, TEACHING HOW TO DO THE “PAT THE PUSS” “JUST OWN IT, LISA! JUST FUCKING OWN IT!” —LISA RINNA TO LISA VANDERPUMP “I’M AT A PLACE WHERE I DON’T QUITE KNOW WHO I WAS MARRIED TO.” —ERIKA “YOU ARE THE BIGGEST BULLY IN HOLLYWOOD AND EVERYONE KNOWS IT.” —KATHY TO LISA RINNA

“I WAS FUCKING ABUSED BY KATHY HILTON.” —**LISA RINNA** “YOU DON’T EXACTLY LIVE LIKE THE QUEEN OF SHEBA. YOU LIVE ON A FUCKING MAIN ROAD.” —**DORIT** “WITCHY-FUCKING-POO! BE QUIET.” —**KYLE TO CARLTON** “HOW THE FUCK DO YOU WIN WITH THIS GROUP?” —**LISA VANDERPUMP** “AM I ANGRY NOW ENOUGH FOR YOU?” —**ERIKA TO CRYSTAL** “YOU WERE BEING A BITCHY FUCKING CUNT.” —**ERIKA TO SUTTON**

SEASON 1

CAST MEMBERS

KYLE RICHARDS / TAYLOR ARMSTRONG
LISA VANDERPUMP / ADRIENNE MALOOF
KIM RICHARDS / CAMILLE GRAMMER

We shot the reunion (deep into the night!) in a grand ballroom of the Millennium Biltmore Hotel in downtown Los Angeles, which ended up being the one and only Beverly Hills *Housewives* reunion we ever shot on location anywhere.

That reunion was when I first felt myself to be the voice of the viewer. Camille was a polarizing housewife, and I was going to have to confront her about the way she had come off on the show. She was already having such a hard time with Twitter, so she knew what was coming. We had discussed on premiere night of *Beverly Hills* how rough the season was going to be for her, but that by the end, when viewers saw how her then-husband, Kelsey Grammer, dumped her unceremoniously, they would come around to her side.

It's just easier to shoot in STUDIOS—you have more CONTROL over the lighting and sound, and they're logistically better suited to our NEEDS.

AIRED

2011

We managed to discuss what KIM meant by saying, "You STOLE my house!"

At the time that we shot this first *Beverly Hills* reunion, though, those episodes hadn't aired. So Camille hadn't begun to feel any level of love or support from the audience. She was especially tender on reunion day. There's a now-viral clip of me reading a long list of horrible adjectives the viewers had called her, while she sits and takes the licks. Oy. This job is not for the fainthearted.

The other BIG issue was the fight that Kyle and Kim had had in the back of the limo. This was especially delicate because the elephant in the room was Kim's sobriety. There were also things they had said relating to their relationship that they regretted and didn't want to go into it at the reunion, making my job all the more difficult! We delved lightly into substance abuse, among other things, and that first reunion set the standard for all *Beverly Hills* reunions to come.

SEASON 2

CAST MEMBERS

KYLE RICHARDS / TAYLOR ARMSTRONG / ADRIENNE MALOOF / BRANDI GLANVILLE / CAMILLE GRAMMER / LISA VANDERPUMP / KIM RICHARDS (NOT PICTURED)

Considering what a heavy season it was for TAYLOR, it's striking how LIGHT and CALM she looks in these pictures.

You get a clear sense of how the fashion standard for reunions has changed in looking at what the women wore to the season two reunion. It definitely started out as simply cocktail attire.

Meanwhile, doesn't the set look straight out of *The Young and the Restless*!

AIRED

2012

"BEING IN A FRIENDSHIP WITH YOU IS LIKE PLAYING CHESS. EVERY MOVE IS VERY CALCULATED." —KYLE TO LISA VANDERPUMP

SEASON 3

CAST MEMBERS

LISA VANDERPUMP / KIM RICHARDS / TAYLOR ARMSTRONG / YOLANDA HADID / BRANDI GLANVILLE / KYLE RICHARDS / ADRIENNE MALOOF (NOT PICTURED)

Looking back on the run of the series, it's IRONIC that LISA VANDERPUMP was the most vocal about Adrienne not attending, given that, years later, she herself did not SHOW.

This is the year that Adrienne Maloof did not show up. I very cavalierly semi-fired her on air, letting it be known that by not coming, she was no longer on the show. And looking back on it now, I think my approach was not very kind.

AIRED

2013

SEASON 4

CAST MEMBERS

KYLE RICHARDS / BRANDI GLANVILLE / KIM RICHARDS / JOYCE GIRAUD / YOLANDA HADID / CARLTON GEBBIA / LISA VANDERPUMP

"I'VE BEEN A VERY GOOD FRIEND TO YOU." —LISA VANDERPUMP

I do wonder what would've happened if Joyce or Carlton had stayed beyond one season. (I still can't get over that we cast someone who publicly identified as a "witch"!) Also, this was the season we seamlessly launched *Vanderpump Rules* out of an episode of *Beverly Hills,* a first for Bravo. The viewers went wild!

AIRED

2014

"YES, AND YOU'VE BEEN A VERY SHITTY FRIEND AT THE SAME TIME."—BRANDI

SEASON 5

CAST MEMBERS

KYLE RICHARDS / LISA VANDERPUMP / LISA RINNA / YOLANDA HADID / EILEEN DAVIDSON / KIM RICHARDS / BRANDI GLANVILLE

"FUCKING CHANGE YOUR DEPENDS CAUSE YOU'RE FULL OF SHIT." —BRANDI

Beverly Hills was already a big hit, but season five launched it into the future with the addition of Eileen and Rinna. Brandi outed me for being attracted to guys in their twenties, and I perhaps wrongly made an analogy comparing Brandi to a puppy, to which she responded, "Fuck you."

AIRED

2015

This was also the year of the iconic AMSTERDAM TRIP!

BRANDI and I were very SPICY at this reunion.

SEASON 6

CAST MEMBERS

LISA RINNA / EILEEN DAVIDSON / KATHRYN EDWARDS / ERIKA JAYNE / YOLANDA HADID / KYLE RICHARDS / LISA VANDERPUMP

This was ERIKA'S first reunion, and I'm not sure I could have PREDICTED then how long she would LAST.

I loved Vanderpump's champagne sequin TOM FORD dress, which wound up on several other housewives as the years passed.

AIRED

2016

"THIS ISN'T A SOAP OPERA, THIS IS REALITY."—KIM TO EILEEN

SEASON 7

CAST MEMBERS

KYLE RICHARDS / LISA VANDERPUMP / DORIT KEMSLEY / EILEEN DAVIDSON / ERIKA JAYNE / LISA RINNA

This reunion became infamous for Kim Richards's return of a bunny wrapped in cellophane that Lisa Rinna had given her, a moment that lives forever in *Housewives* lore. I knew that Kim had the bunny with her that day and wanted to return it, which sounded to me, as a producer, like a deliciously dramatic spectacle! However, I never could have imagined how awkward and amusing it would be. Kim's delivery of the bunny return was so spot-on and dramatic and odd, made especially unique by the loud crinkling of the cellophane. When she brought it out, I immediately turned to Kyle, who was furiously trying to keep herself from laughing, which of course brought me to near laughter. I took the bunny at the end of that day to put in The Clubhouse for posterity, and years later, Anderson Cooper and I brought it on tour.

When I saw that LISA RINNA had dropped a single TEAR, I knew I needed to redirect my emotion, since this gesture had not landed HUMOROUSLY for Lisa.

AIRED

2017

Me and Anderson pictured in a HELICOPTER to Atlantic City. Every time we brought the BUNNY onstage, audiences went NUTS, just like they did when they saw that reunion.

SEASON 8

CAST MEMBERS

LISA VANDERPUMP / DORIT KEMSLEY / ERIKA JAYNE / LISA RINNA / TEDDI MELLENCAMP ARROYAVE / KYLE RICHARDS

"I DO TREAT YOU THE SAME; I'M RUDE TO EVERYBODY." —ERIKA

AIRED

2018

I absolutely love the OUTFITS, probably because everyone looks like they're going to STUDIO 54!

SEASON 9

CAST MEMBERS

KYLE RICHARDS /
TEDDI MELLENCAMP ARROYAVE /
DORIT KEMSLEY / DENISE RICHARDS /
ERIKA JAYNE / LISA RINNA

What stood out for me was Camille's short but fiery appearance. I remember her removing her dress and microphone in one fell swoop as she stormed off the set. I've never seen anything like it!

Look at DORIT, with her head full of BARRETTES! This is one of many incredibly DRAMATIC HAIR looks.

AIRED

2019

"DID YOU HAVE A NOSE JOB?"—ANDY "NO! MAKEUP CAN DO WONDERS!"—DORIT

SEASON 10

CAST MEMBERS

LISA RINNA / DORIT KEMSLEY / KYLE RICHARDS / GARCELLE BEAUVAIS / TEDDI MELLENCAMP ARROYAVE / ERIKA JAYNE / SUTTON STRACKE / DENISE RICHARDS

This is the COVID virtual reunion. (Not our first, that distinction went to *The Real Housewives of Atlanta*.) The picture above is from a TECH TEST the day before we taped, which is why everyone's wearing NORMAL CLOTHES.

Looks like I was testing out the JACKET I was going to wear.

This was probably my LEAST FAVORITE *Beverly Hills* reunion, not only because it was virtual, but also because it lacked the humor and levity that usually balance some of the DRAMA.

I was on the EAST COAST in Michael Davies's (executive producer of *WWHL*) BASEMENT in Bridgehampton, while the women were each in their HOMES.

AIRED

2020

The day after testing our Zoom shots, we shot the reunion. It's so funny now to see the intense glam for a virtual reunion, specifically Kyle's and Lisa's. But I get it—there were no opportunities to dress during the pandemic! The big drama that day was between Denise and the rest of the women relating to the allegations that she and Brandi had had an affair. It was Garcelle's first reunion and I remember feeling badly because she had to do it virtually and also because things got so ugly between Denise and some of the women. I was such a fan of Garcelle's and didn't want this virtual reunion to taint her feelings about returning to the show. Before shooting, there was a lot of discord about whether Brandi should attend that reunion, and about whether Denise *would,* with both conversations going into the night. We shot until after midnight East Coast time and afterward I remember just sitting alone deep into the night with a much-needed tequila as all the women's voices rang in my head.

SEASON 11

CAST MEMBERS

KYLE RICHARDS / GARCELLE BEAUVAIS / SUTTON STRACKE / CRYSTAL MINKOFF / DORIT KEMSLEY / LISA RINNA / ERIKA JAYNE

As you can see from Erika's facial expression, this was her first time under questioning about all that had happened with her then-estranged husband, Tom Girardi. That reunion required the most advance preparation since I had faced the Salahis in the one and only reunion for *The Real Housewives of D.C.* I felt an incredible amount of pressure from the viewers to get answers from Erika and to hold her accountable. In fact, as we were getting ready for the day, I told Erika I was going "to put her on the grill and turn up the heat," an exchange that appeared in the super tease and in the show, and which I later regretted because it just felt too aggressive on my part. I apologized for that years later, and she accepted. Of all the housewives, she is one with a unique understanding and perspective on the experience—she's able to see it from thirty thousand feet in the air. (By the way, I was proud of my interview with her, which was thorough and fair. My ten years at CBS News, and years of previous reunions, trained me well for it.)

The set that year was modeled after KATHY HILTON'S BACKYARD, a reference that seemed to be lost on the GRANDE DAME of Beverly Hills when I asked her about it.

AIRED

2021

"I KNOW WHAT YOU MAKE ON THIS SHOW. IT AIN'T BAD."—ANDY

"I GAVE EVERY PAYCHECK TO MY HUSBAND."—ERIKA

The look ERIKA'S giving me is so evocative of the tough matter-of-fact demeanor she took on throughout what turned out to be two hours of really DIRECT questioning.

SEASON 12

CAST MEMBERS

LISA RINNA / ERIKA JAYNE / DORIT KEMSLEY / CRYSTAL MINKOFF / SUTTON STRACKE / GARCELLE BEAUVAIS / KYLE RICHARDS / DIANA JENKINS (NOT PICTURED)

During the TAPING, it became clear to me and I think to some of the other producers that LISA RINNA'S time on the show was coming to an END. Clearly she had the same feeling because she texted us all at midnight that very night QUITTING the show.

As the evening wore on it became evident just how fractured KYLE'S relationship with her SISTER was and that they were not going to be able to mend things because I hadn't seen Kyle that upset ever . . . and I've seen her pretty UPSET.

AIRED

2022

This reunion was notable because it came off of Lisa Rinna and Kathy Hilton's epic battle after the cast trip to Aspen. I was prepared for an incredibly dramatic day, but a few things still surprised me. For starters, Kathy Hilton came in with guns blazing and landed some memorable zingers. She'd always seemed conflict-averse to me so I had had low expectations for how she would stand up for herself.

SEASON 13

CAST MEMBERS

SUTTON STRACKE / GARCELLE BEAUVAIS / CRYSTAL MINKOFF / ANNEMARIE WILEY / DORIT KEMSLEY / ERIKA JAYNE / KYLE RICHARDS

This season was the third consecutive reunion where I yawned while Dorit was speaking! The prior two times Dorit asked, "Am I boring you?" But this time she simply said, "Don't you dare!" I quickly apologized, but what can I say? It was a long day! Dorit is actually not the first *Beverly Hills* housewife I have yawned at. Yolanda Hadid got it, too! Whoops!

I took these photos just as the women were ARRIVING for the day, and each of their faces look like the CAT that ate the canary. Why? DORIT had just entered the set, and they were all reacting in amazement to her WILD ENSEMBLE.

AIRED

2024

"DON'T TALK TO ME ABOUT NOT SHARING MY LIFE! YOU BOUGHT A HORSE THIS SEASON AND YOU HAVE A DATING COACH. GIVE ME A BREAK!"—KYLE TO SUTTON

SEASON 14

CAST MEMBERS

DORIT KEMSLEY / BOZOMA SAINT JOHN / ERIKA JAYNE / GARCELLE BEAUVAIS / SUTTON STRACKE / KYLE RICHARDS

It makes me SAD looking at how happy GARCELLE is here at the beginning of the day, knowing how UPSET she would be ten hours LATER.

AIRED

2025

I would love to know what KYLE was thinking in this moment, because she looks really AMUSED.

SEASON 15

CAST MEMBERS

DORIT KEMSLEY / BOZOMA SAINT JOHN / RACHEL ZOE / AMANDA FRANCES / SUTTON STRACKE / ERIKA JAYNE / KYLE RICHARDS

This was a standout season for newcomer Rachel Zoe, and in the days leading up to the reunion, I wondered what she would wear. She killed it, as always. But how about Jennifer Tilly's Balmain dress, featuring an image of Jennifer Tilly? She was worried it wouldn't be a good "sitting down dress," but it served her well.

RACHEL ZOE, I DIE.

JENNIFER TILLY advised SUTTON to show more CLEAVAGE this season and it looks like she took her advice at the reunion. I thought Sutton looked the best she has looked in her six seasons on the show.

AIRED

2026

TILLY on TILLY.

This was a reunion that I entered hoping that friendships would be restored between either Dorit and Kyle or Dorit and Erika. Sadly, we closed the day in a worse place for both. The other headline of the season was the “Money Queen” Amanda Frances, who didn’t back down for the entire day. And I have to respect her for that! As always, the women looked outstanding.

UPFRONTS & PARTIES

Every year networks gather their biggest talent and put on a dog and pony show for advertisers in order to generate interest in their programming. These are called the "upfronts" and Bravo's were always the most fun. They're a great opportunity to see seemingly incongruous groups of housewives and Bravolebrities interacting behind the scenes. They were BravoCon before it existed!

For many years, Bravo scheduled their "Summer by Bravo" ad campaign shoots on the day before the big upfront, since all the talent would be in the same city. This Summer by Bravo campaign had us all competing in the Olympics.

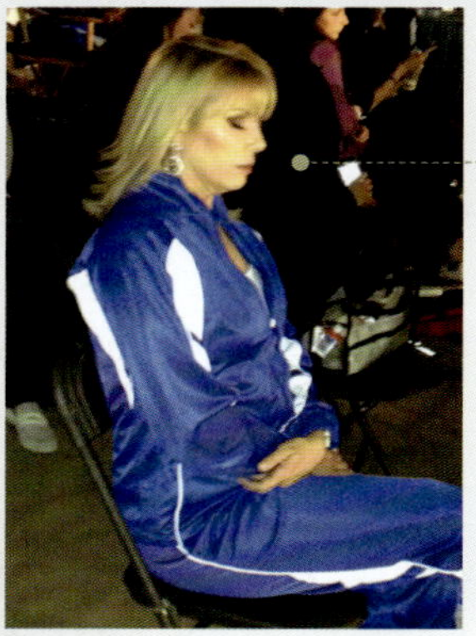

Ramona Singer, who is always on brand, fell asleep sitting up during the shoot, something she did a few years later at the season seven reunion.

This is a Summer by Bravo campaign where the concept was that we were all at the same party. It's so fun seeing Nene Leakes and Kim Zolciak-Biermann with Tom Colicchio.

I love this group photo of Shereé Whitfield, Nene Leakes, Teresa Giudice, Lisa Wu, Jacqueline Laurita, Bethenny Frankel, and Kandi Burruss, a murderer's row of iconic housewives, all early in their runs on their shows and Bethenny with child.

In 2012, we made our upfronts into an episode of *Watch What Happens Live,* which filmed in SoHo and featured tables full of Bravolebrities. Here you can see the *Flipping Out* group mixing with the *Orange County* housewives, and the Atlanta girls talking to Madison Hildebrand from *Million Dollar Listing Los Angeles.*

JERSEY in the house!

Here are the *BEVERLY HILLS* girls.

I love this selfie with housewives from *Miami, Potomac, Atlanta, Beverly Hills,* and *Jersey,* along with *Million Dollar Listing,* backstage at Radio City Music Hall.

This was from a *Family Feud*–style game we played onstage. All I remember is that everyone was talking over one another, which happens to be the story of my life on Bravo.

This feels like HISTORY to me! If you're reading this book, you feel me . . .

This is a photo from a party in L.A. taken on my BlackBerry! Lynne Curtin, Gretchen Rossi, Kelly Bensimon, Lauri Peterson, Shereé Whitfield, and Nene Leakes. This feels like olden times—so low-tech!

After the upfront, we would usually all gather at what was then the Trump SoHo for drinks. Kim Richards, Kandi Burruss, Kyle Richards, Melissa Gorga, Vicki Gunvalson, and Sonja Morgan feel like they'd make an outstanding cast for *Ultimate Girls Trip* (a show we hadn't yet come up with . . .).

Here is a great pic of Cynthia Bailey, Nene Leakes, Jenni Pulos, and Kenya Moore. I remember Kenya and Brandi Glanville getting into a playful back-and-forth instigated by Jeff Lewis. One can only imagine what it was about . . .

KENTUCKY DERBY

In 2010, I was sent to the Kentucky Derby with Dina Manzo and Jeff Lewis and Jenni Pulos to host a show the day before the race. We were young and innocent-ish and had an absolute ball.

This is also the weekend I met Jerry O'Connell and Rebecca Romijn for the first time. And we became fast friends. We partied so hard I believe that was the weekend Jerry O'Connell decided to get sober.

Also JOHNNY WEIR.

PHOTO SHOOTS

Backstage at a photo shoot for *The Hollywood Reporter* with *The Real Housewives of Beverly Hills* in 2011.

Backstage for an *Advocate* magazine cover shoot that featured me, Nene Leakes, Bethenny Frankel, and Dina Manzo, dressed as fifties versions of housewives. I remember being so excited to be on the cover of the *Advocate*, only to discover that I'd be dressed like an old-timey dad. (I wasn't ready to be a dad yet—I wanted to be CUTE.)

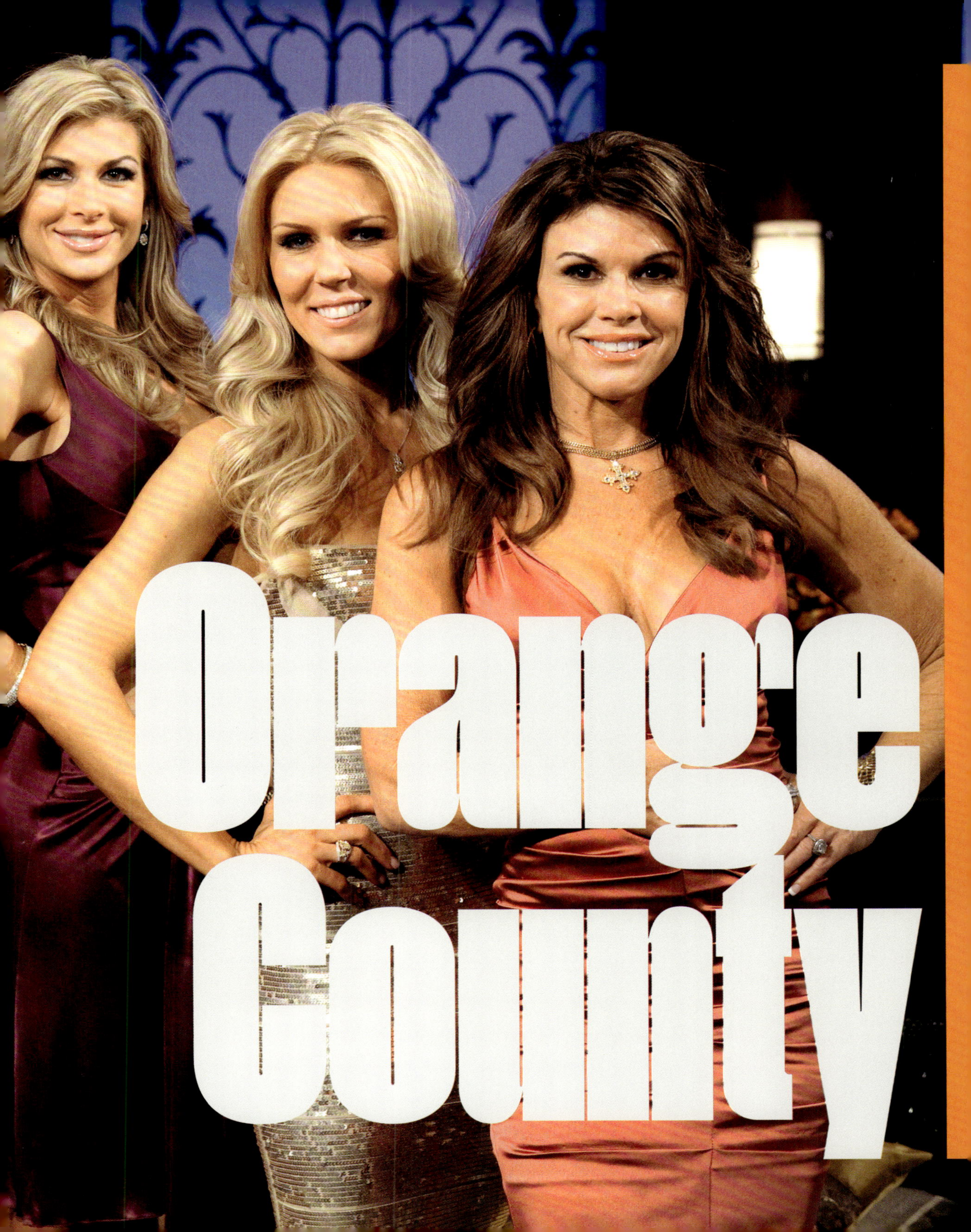
Orange
County

THE very first *Housewives* reunion took place without me and also, notably, without any drama. We put the women in Vicki's backyard, sitting around a big-screen TV, reacting to clips of themselves. It feels very quaint now.

After season two, Bravo suggested extending the interactive *Top Chef After Show* I was doing on BravoTV.com (a mild hit by 2006 standards!) into a reunion format for the *Housewives*. The show would be me asking questions submitted by the viewers through the site. I had always dreamed of being on air and this would be my prime-time debut, a huge opportunity. We filmed in an L.A. studio. Four things stick in my memory about that day: (1) My Afro was out of control; (2) as we were getting ready to shoot, Jeana Keough said, "I guess this is a good sign for the show. The fact that we're getting a reunion and shooting it here, we must be doing well?"; (3) I asked a provocative, some might say RUDE, viewer question, and that boundary-pushing style of questioning went on to become my trademark

ISO 100
ISO 100
ISO 100

ISO 100
ISO 100

ISO 100
ISO 100

(in this instance, it was: "Lauri, how does it feel being compared to a transvestite?"); and (4) my instincts as a producer at the time weren't yet honed. Jeana at one point started to cry and instead of leaning into it, I suggested we take a break until she got herself together. Talk about missing a moment!

I always saw *Orange County* as the *Knots Landing* of the *Housewives* franchise, meaning they were the most grounded in suburban life and relatability. That extends to the fashions of these reunions, especially for the first half of the pictures you're about to see. Another highlight of *Orange County* reunions is that for many years Vicki would wink at me throughout the day during tapings, which always brought a smile to my face.

"YOU ARE PSYCHOTIC, JESUS JUGS! YOU'RE PSYCHOTIC!" —**TAMRA** "I SAID I'M SORRY. DO YOU WANT ME TO POP A VEIN?" —**HEATHER** "THAT'S MY OPINION!" —**TAMRA** "I DON'T HAVE PROOF HE'S NOT FAKING CANCER AND I DON'T HAVE PROOF HE IS." —**VICKI** "SHE'S LIKE A FART. SHE'S SILENT BUT DEADLY." —**KELLY ABOUT VICKI** "YOU'RE GOING TO DROP A BOMB ABOUT CPS AND YOU DON'T EVEN KNOW MY KIDS' NAMES?" —**GINA KIRSCHENHEITER** "WE GET CALLED TRANSVESTITES ALL THE TIME." —**LAURI PETERSON**

“I FEEL MORE COMFORTABLE WHEN A MAN IS RUNNING MY COUNTRY.” —ALEXIS “IF EVERYONE SAYS YOU’RE DEAD, IT’S TIME TO LIE DOWN.” —HEATHER “I THINK THE WHOLE WORLD LIKES ME.” —KELLY “WE ARE ALL GOOD PEOPLE. WE JUST GOT A LITTLE DERAILED.” —VICKI “CAN WE CHANGE OUR COUCH NOW?” —TAMRA “I’M NOT GOING TO START YELLING THIS TIME.” —SHANNON “YOU’RE YELLING RIGHT NOW.” —EMILY “EVERY TRASH CAN NEEDS A LID AND JOHN JANSSEN FOUND HIS.” —EMILY

SEASON 2

CAST MEMBERS

JEANA KEOUGH / LAURI PETERSON / JO DE LA ROSA / VICKI GUNVALSON / TAMMY KNICKERBOCKER

AIRED

2007

This is still so WEIRD, looking back on it: the DIRECTOR'S CHAIRS, the sky-blue backdrop, and the ladies in MALL-WEAR. I was BURNING UP in that velvet jacket.

I think JACKIE WARNER was there from Work Out so that PRESS could get some good SHOTS of her—RANDOM!

"ALL 5. ALL 5. EVERYBODY RAISE THEIR HAND. 100% HERE."—VICKI, ABOUT BOOB JOBS

SEASON 3

CAST MEMBERS

QUINN FRY / VICKI GUNVALSON / TAMMY KNICKERBOCKER / TAMRA JUDGE / JEANA KEOUGH / LAURI PETERSON

AIRED

2008

I have VAGUE memories of this one. VICKI was constantly winking at me.

"I WILL NEVER IN MY ENTIRE LIFE DO THAT AGAIN." —VICKI ON HER "WOOHOO" SCREAM

We were still in the QUAINT DAYS here.

I always had a SOFT SPOT for LAURI and especially on this day when she reminisced about her gay brother who passed away from AIDS.

SEASON 4

CAST MEMBERS

JEANA KEOUGH / GRETCHEN ROSSI / LYNNE CURTIN / LAURI PETERSON / VICKI GUNVALSON / TAMRA JUDGE

This was the first *Orange County* reunion where I sat in the middle, with two couches of housewives on each side. Lynne Curtin on the end seemed to be off with the fairies. Though I was by this point well-versed in getting the most drama out of reunions. Jeana continued to shy away from conflict, in contrast to most housewives. Her instinct was like mine on that first reunion—to shut down drama, which is probably great for real life but not so great when you're making a reunion show.

This reunion SET *is* the BLUEPRINT that now feels second NATURE for any and all reunions.

This was TAMRA'S first reunion and she arrived with a bang, declaring herself the "HOTTEST housewife."

AIRED

2009

"YOU'RE SUCH A FUCKING VICTIM, AREN'T YOU?" —TAMRA TO GRETCHEN

Sorry for the HORRIBLE QUALITY— this is circa my DIGITAL CAMERA!

SEASON 5

CAST MEMBERS

GRETCHEN ROSSI / ALEXIS BELLINO / LYNNE CURTIN / VICKI GUNVALSON / TAMRA JUDGE

This is one of the first reunions that featured an appearance by Slade Smiley and, years later, went viral on TikTok. Slade said that after the second season HE made the decision to leave the show, so I reminded him that since he and Jo had broken up, there was no reason for him to be featured on *Real Housewives.* Through the years, I always appreciated the men taking part in the reunions to stand by their wives.

Worth noting that every year GRETCHEN showed up for a reunion, I told her that she looked "VERY PAGEANT." I LOVE that about her, and I think she loved hearing it.

AIRED

2010

"THE IMPLICATION IS THAT TAMRA IS WHITE TRASH." —ANDY

SEASON 6

CAST MEMBERS

GRETCHEN ROSSI / ALEXIS BELLINO / PEGGY TANOUS / VICKI GUNVALSON / TAMRA JUDGE

Much more DRAMA surrounding SLADE Smiley.

SLADE didn't stay for the whole reunion, but this was the ONLY picture I took!

Not to get too intellectual, but this is an interesting one to look back on because it was so much about the role of women in relationships, in their households, and in society at large, with Alexis taking the more conservative role and Vicki and Tamra, the more progressive.

AIRED

2011

SEASON 7

CAST MEMBERS

VICKI GUNVALSON / ALEXIS BELLINO / HEATHER DUBROW / GRETCHEN ROSSI / TAMRA JUDGE

I used to FILM the women's SHOES for bravotv.com. Feels VERY pre-TikTok!

This year saw the addition of Heather Dubrow, who came in with a bang. Also, this was the birth of the term "Jesus Jugs," a name I'd assumed Alexis would take offense to but wore with pride. This is one of the things I love about the housewives: their ability to laugh at themselves.

AIRED

2012

Lots of PAGEANT HAIR at this reunion.

SEASON 8

CAST MEMBERS

GRETCHEN ROSSI / HEATHER DUBROW / LYDIA MCLAUGHLIN / ALEXIS BELLINO / TAMRA JUDGE / VICKI GUNVALSON

This was the reunion that featured Brooks, who was still very much with Vicki and very much under scrutiny by Vicki's family and the other housewives. Briana was there to very firmly advocate for her mother. If I wasn't already a Briana fan,

"I'M A MONOGAMOUS GIRL." —VICKI

AIRED

2013

I certainly left that day loving her. I'm always impressed watching the housewives' kids grow into the best versions of themselves and often the calmer, more reasonable versions of their mothers. Briana is no exception.

SEASON 9

CAST MEMBERS

SHANNON BEADOR / VICKI GUNVALSON / LIZZIE ROVSEK / HEATHER DUBROW / TAMRA JUDGE

Shannon entered this season as a very CONSERVATIVE Orange County wife. She's had quite an EVOLUTION!

"SHUT UP! GOD! JUST GO SIT OVER THERE!"—TAMRA

Brooks was featured in this reunion and I still chuckle at the way he exited the set: He went up a flight of stairs that led nowhere. So while the exit may have looked interesting, he was, again, going nowhere. That's very apt.

AIRED

2014

This is the reunion that birthed the "THAT'S MY OPINION!" clip that's since gone very VIRAL. I have no real recollection of it happening, but it always makes me SMILE.

SEASON 10

CAST MEMBERS

SHANNON BEADOR / TAMRA JUDGE / MEGHAN KING EDMONDS / HEATHER DUBROW / VICKI GUNVALSON

"I THINK MY MOM HAS STOCKHOLM SYNDROME." —BRIANA CULBERSON

This was the year that Vicki and Brooks were finally broken up, and we rolled into the show a one-on-one with Brooks from the *Watch What Happens Live* studio, in which he essentially copped to fabricating parts of his story. You can't make this stuff up! Briana, as always, was the voice of reason in the group.

AIRED

2015

SEASON 11

CAST MEMBERS

VICKI GUNVALSON / KELLY DODD / MEGHAN KING EDMONDS / HEATHER DUBROW / TAMRA JUDGE / SHANNON BEADOR

This was KELLY DODD'S first season, and I think it's fair to say she didn't win all the women over, but I was highly AMUSED! Her self-confidence was through the ROOF.

AIRED

2016

SEASON 12

CAST MEMBERS

TAMRA JUDGE / SHANNON BEADOR / MEGHAN KING EDMONDS / PEGGY SULAHIAN / LYDIA MCLAUGHLIN / KELLY DODD / VICKI GUNVALSON

The "Tres Amigas" went off course this season but reconciled at the reunion with a group hug that stunned everyone, including me. The road getting there was rough, though, with Vicki quitting the show mid-reunion, but happily ultimately deciding to stay. This was the first of many times a housewife would quit the show in vain at a reunion.

AIRED

2017

SEASON 13

CAST MEMBERS

SHANNON BEADOR / VICKI GUNVALSON / EMILY SIMPSON / GINA KIRSCHENHEITER / KELLY DODD / TAMRA JUDGE

This was the OFFICIAL END of Shannon's marriage and the beginning of her JOURNEY as a SINGLE woman. She seemed battle-weary.

AIRED

2018

SEASON 14

CAST MEMBERS

KELLY DODD / EMILY SIMPSON / BRAUNWYN WINDHAM-BURKE / GINA KIRSCHENHEITER / TAMRA JUDGE / SHANNON BEADOR / VICKI GUNVALSON

As a Vicki fan, I found this reunion a bit tough to swallow. She was a "friend" this season and was only out for a portion of the time, which predictably didn't sit well with the OG of the *OC*. She had a few moments in this reunion (insisting she hadn't auditioned for the

“WE NEED TO ELEVATE THIS CAST. IT’S A DISASTER. I’M EMBARRASSED TO BE PART OF IT.” —VICKI

AIRED

2019

show, being agitated about not being on set for the toast at the end of taping, deriding the quality of the newest housewife, Braunwyn) that were as close to a real-life version of *The Comeback* as I’ve seen during my entire time with this franchise. Of course, all those moments all made it into the show.

SEASON 15

CAST MEMBERS

KELLY DODD / SHANNON BEADOR / ELIZABETH LYN VARGAS / EMILY SIMPSON / GINA KIRSCHENHEITER / BRAUNWYN WINDHAM-BURKE

It was a few days before Christmas and I barely made it due to a snowstorm on the East Coast. But I was able to spend the holiday in California and even brought my son along. It was Kelly Dodd's last reunion; much has been said about Kelly's exit and she has alleged that she was fired for her political views, but the truth is that the audience turned on her in a very big way. A large group of housewives, podcasters, and bloggers refused to cover the show as a kind of boycott of her

This was the first COVID reunion we did in PERSON and it was shot (socially distanced) on a stage in a THEATER in L.A.

AIRED

2021

This season marked Braunwyn's FULL transition into a LESBIAN—check out her COMBAT BOOTS.

behavior on social media. It was an unfortunate end to an outspoken and often hysterical *Orange County* housewife. There is a moment on the reunion when I ask Kelly if she's afraid of being on the wrong side of history; I wish I hadn't gone there because for many people, she was on the right side of history. We feature housewives of every political affiliation, and that's what makes the show—much like our country—great. If everyone believed the same thing, it would be pretty boring.

SEASON 16

CAST MEMBERS

HEATHER DUBROW / GINA KIRSCHENHEITER / JEN ARMSTRONG / NOELLA BERGENER / EMILY SIMPSON / SHANNON BEADOR

This reunion was a dramatic end to a semi-lackluster season. I remember going into the day wondering what we would get and leaving feeling energized by the women. This was also Heather's big return.

The beginning of a whole NEW LOOK for SHANNON (curly long hair!).

AIRED

2022

I LOVED the set, which celebrated ICONIC sites in Orange County like the HUNTINGTON BEACH PIER and the GATES from the show's opener.

SEASON 17

CAST MEMBERS

HEATHER DUBROW / GINA KIRSCHENHEITER / JENNIFER PEDRANTI / EMILY SIMPSON / SHANNON BEADOR / TAMRA JUDGE

"HOW MANY POUNDS OF HAIR WOULD YOU SAY ARE ON TOP OF YOUR HEAD?" —ANDY

This was Tamra's return to the show and also the first reunion we did on the Sony soundstage with a huge projection behind us. The set knocked all our socks off. After we got over that, though, the women were at one another's throats for almost the entire day.

AIRED

2023

"NOT AS MUCH AS TERESA'S HAIR FOR HER WEDDING." —SHANNON

SEASON 18

CAST MEMBERS

TAMRA JUDGE / EMILY SIMPSON / HEATHER DUBROW / KATIE GINELLA / JENNIFER PEDRANTI / GINA KIRSCHENHEITER / SHANNON BEADOR

This reunion was Shannon Beador versus the world as Alexis returned to the show, now dating Shannon's ex-boyfriend. There was a moment that I still look back on with a chuckle, when Alexis was kind of bragging to Shannon about her career on television. Once again, it was reminiscent of *The Comeback*.

AIRED

2024

SEASON 19

CAST MEMBERS

JENNIFER PEDRANTI / EMILY SIMPSON / SHANNON BEADOR / GRETCHEN ROSSI / KATIE GINELLA / HEATHER DUBROW / GINA KIRSCHENHEITER / TAMRA JUDGE

"BECAUSE YOU'RE TAMRA GRUDGE. YOU HAVE ALL THE GRUDGES." —SHANNON

This was the season GRETCHEN RETURNED, reigniting OLD FEUDS with Tamra that probably should have remained in the PAST.

AIRED

2025

Salt Lake City

SALT *Lake City* reunions have been over-the-top and memorable, and not just because of the drama. The sets themselves have been an almost hallucinogenic journey through *Housewives* scene spectacles. We have had the most memorable sets in any franchise—from snowscapes to shipwrecks to Sprinter vans to Santorini! What a spectacle.

ISO 100
ISO 100
Real Housewives
ISO 100 3
ISO 100 4

ISO 100
ISO 100
ISO 100 3
ISO 100 4

ISO 100
ISO 100
ISO 100 3
ISO 100 4

ISO 100
ISO 100
ISO 100 3
ISO 100 4

ISO 100
ISO 100
ISO 100 3
ISO 100 4

ISO 100
ISO 100
ISO 100 3
ISO 100 4

"WHITNEY AND HEATHER. BAD WEATHER. TORNADO. SPIN THE TRUTH. DESTROY!" —**LISA**

"THE MORE YOU TALK, THE MORE YOU CRUCIFY YOURSELF." —**HEATHER**

"HEATHER, I WOULD BE FINE BEING ON AN ISLAND ALONE." —**LISA**

"WELL FIRST OF ALL, I'M NOT IN MY FIFTIES." —**JEN**

"I HAVEN'T BEEN THE ONE TRYING TO GET ON THIS SHOW FOR THREE YEARS." —**MEREDITH TO ANGIE K.**

"YOU FALL ASLEEP?" —**ANDY**

"NO, ANDY . . . I . . ." —**MARY COSBY**

"IT'S OKAY THAT YOU DID! IT'S HAPPENED BEFORE."—**ANDY**
"I DON'T REMEMBER."—**MARY COSBY**
"DON'T TALK ABOUT MY CHURCH! NO ONE IS BRINGING UP YOUR ALCOHOL!"—**MARY COSBY TO LISA**
"NO MATTER WHERE I'M GOING, I HAVE GLAM EVERY DAY."—**LISA**
"SHE NEEDS A MUTE BUTTON."—**MARY COSBY**
"IF I WERE A CREDIT CARD, I'D SUE YOU FOR IDENTITY THEFT."—**LISA (TO ANGIE K.)**
"I'M INNOCENT, AND I NEED TO TELL MY STORY."—**JEN**

SEASON 1

CAST MEMBERS

JEN SHAH / LISA BARLOW /
MARY COSBY / MEREDITH MARKS /
WHITNEY ROSE / HEATHER GAY

MARY M. COSBY became the second housewife in reunion history (after Ramona Singer) to FALL ASLEEP.

The first *Salt Lake City* reunion was during COVID and the women were socially distanced. It featured lots of sequins and snow, always a great combination. That reunion birthed the “bad weather” nickname Lisa gave Whitney and Heather.

AIRED

2021

Half the CREW got COVID in the days that followed. WORTH IT!

SEASON 2

CAST MEMBERS

JEN SHAH / HEATHER GAY / WHITNEY ROSE / MEREDITH MARKS / JENNIE NGUYEN / LISA BARLOW

The season two reunion was my first opportunity to question Jen Shah after her arrest. I was excited and anxious for answers because she hadn't spoken about the charges publicly, and I didn't know what to expect. She looked me in the eyes and tearfully proclaimed her innocence and convincingly advocated for those who have been wrongly prosecuted for crimes. Seven months later, she pled guilty to conspiracy to commit wire fraud and was sentenced to six and a

I certainly didn't have JEN SHAH dressed like a SHOWGIRL in feathers and dangling RHINESTONES on my bingo card as I QUESTIONED her about facing federal CHARGES.

AIRED

2022

half years in prison. Jen was so convincing with her tears, and I was rooting for her so hard. When it was really clear that she had committed these crimes, I was especially disappointed. We have not spoken since. Also, Mary didn't show up to the reunion! I remember calling and texting her until the morning of taping, and all she would tell me was that "God knew whether [she] was coming." And the producers and I really wanted God to give us the answer. The empty seat was the response.

SEASON 3

CAST MEMBERS

WHITNEY ROSE / LISA BARLOW / MEREDITH MARKS / HEATHER GAY

This was our worst *SLC* reunion! It was like the air had left the room. Jen Shah was about to be sentenced and the women, who all had strong opinions about their convicted costar, were markedly clammed up about her crimes in front of the camera, which was incredibly frustrating. It seemed that no one really wanted to come out with

The season three reunion featured a PIRATE SHIPWRECK in a SNOWSTORM motif (DON'T ASK) and all of us exiting a SPRINTER VAN to get onto set.

AIRED

2023

an opinion about her, even though they all had them. This was also the season of Heather's black eye and all the confusion surrounding that situation. She was unprepared to tell us where she got it (later she alleged it was Shah) and was seemingly not in a good place personally, and that came through in the reunion.

SEASON 4

CAST MEMBERS

HEATHER GAY / LISA BARLOW / ANGIE KATSANEVAS / WHITNEY ROSE / MEREDITH MARKS / MONICA GARCIA

The season four reunion was highly anticipated due to the explosive finale in which Monica Garcia's association with the troll account "Reality Von Tease" was revealed. This was the first time since the cast trip that the women would be confronting Monica. I loved Monica as a housewife and was rooting for her to apologize and find

"YOU CALLED ME A TRAMPOLINE WITH EYES." —MEREDITH "THAT WAS A COMPLIMENT." —ANGIE K.

AIRED

2024

By the END of the reunion, it seemed CLEAR to the producers and me that MONICA would only be a one-season housewife.

some middle ground with the ladies that would allow her to continue on the show. Going into the reunion, I felt like she was most likely to be able to make amends with Whitney Rose. Unfortunately, she brought a "burn book" as a prop that was dramatic for television, but didn't help her make any inroads with the women.

SEASON 5

CAST MEMBERS

LISA BARLOW / HEATHER GAY / MEREDITH MARKS / WHITNEY ROSE / BRONWYN NEWPORT / MARY COSBY / ANGIE KATSANEVAS

"FROM BENCH-WARMING BITCH TO FIRST CHAIR."—ANGIE K.

This was the season that Mary emerged as a fan favorite and an unlikely voice of reason in the group.

"IF WE CAN JUST HELP ONE PERSON THEN WE'LL TELL OUR TRUTH."—MARY COSBY

AIRED

2025

ANGIE K. really broke out as a housewife this season. After being DERIDED at the season four reunion for being on the end of the COUCH, she almost CRIED when she was placed next to me.

SEASON 6

CAST MEMBERS

LISA BARLOW / MEREDITH MARKS / MARY COSBY / WHITNEY ROSE / BRITANI BATEMAN / ANGIE KATSANEVAS / HEATHER GAY / BRONWYN NEWPORT

We went back to Greece for the season six *SLC* reunion. I loved the set. I loved how the ladies looked. I will never get used to Bronwyn with long hair, but her emotions about separating from Todd really touched me. This was also the first reunion that I ever walked out of myself. I was just sick of them talking over one another, but of course, once I was two steps off the set, I became annoyed because my real goal is to finish shooting and have a great day. And without me, that couldn't happen. I quickly returned, making my walk-off as much a flop as many that had preceded me.

Two things happen during breaks in filming reunions: One is that there's a STAMPEDE of HAIR and MAKEUP personnel touching up the women. P.S.: Shout-out to Brooks Marks.

AIRED

2026

The second thing that occurs is the HAIR and MAKEUP folks become personal PHOTOGRAPHERS, who even bring their own lighting. MASTERPIECES must be saved for POSTERITY.

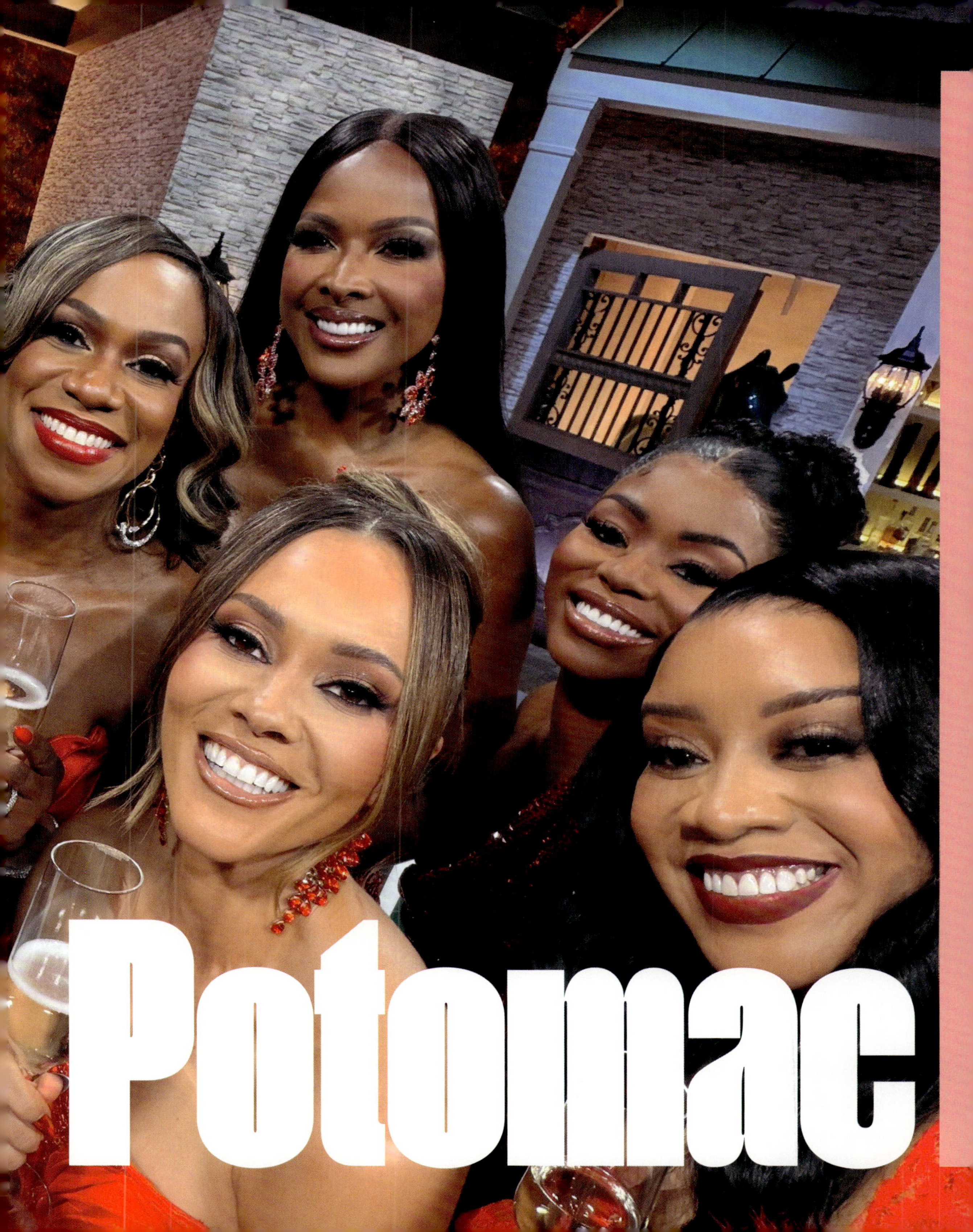

Potomac

POTOMAC reunions are some of my favorites because they're always both super dramatic and funny. These ladies know how to read, and they have a lot going on in their personal lives. We've had more success dressing the *Potomac* women in color schematics than we have in any other city. They rise to the occasion every year.

“WHO IS ANDREW WITH A MISSING DIGIT?” —**KAREN**

“I DIDN’T NEED A LESSON, LOVE. AND YOU CAN’T TEACH IT.” —**KAREN**

“ARE YOU ONE OF THE WOMEN? DO YOU HAVE A DRESS ON?” —**KAREN TO MICHAEL DARBY**

“GRANDE DAME OF NOT A DAMN THING.” —**CHARRISSE**

“THE MAN YOU LAY WITH IS ITCHING. TAKE A TEST.” —**CANDIACE**

“AND YOU’RE A HOUSE TROLLOP. BE QUIET.” —**CANDIACE**

"I GOT THEM IN MY LITTLE RECEIPT BOOK RIGHT HERE." —**MONIQUE** "HE'S A RADIO PERSONALITY." —**MIA** "CONGRATULATIONS TO KAREN. HER GERITOL JUST KICKED IN." —**GIZELLE** "SHE'S NOT A HOUSEWIFE, SHE'S A HOUSE DAUGHTER. THAT'S GREAT." —**ASHLEY** "PEOPLE SAY YOU HAVE A BOYFRIEND. DO I TALK ABOUT THAT? BLUE EYES OR WHATEVER HIS NAME IS." —**CHARRISSE** "SHE'S VICIOUS AND I AM A DARLING." —**KAREN** "LIES!" —**GIZELLE**

SEASON 1

CAST MEMBERS

GIZELLE BRYANT / ROBYN DIXON / ASHLEY DARBY / CHARRISSE JACKSON-JORDAN / KATIE ROST / KAREN HUGER

"AND I ABSOLUTELY LOVE ME SOME KAREN. IF YOU DON'T KNOW THAT. I'M IN LOVE WITH THIS AND THE MOLE AIN'T GOING NOWHERE."—KAREN

"AND GO GET YOUR MEDS ADJUSTED, BABY." —KAREN TO ASHLEY

AIRED

2016

KAREN really DOMINATED the first *Potomac* reunion.

Karen had so many great lines and never broke a sweat. That version of Karen continues through the run of *Potomac*. There was a point in this first reunion when she asked Michael Darby, "Are you one of the women? Do you have a dress on?" I always get sensitive when the women say stuff like that to the men because we've actually invited the men to participate, then they say "yes" and the women castigate them for showing up.

SEASON 2

CAST MEMBERS

GIZELLE BRYANT / ROBYN DIXON / CHARRISSE JACKSON-JORDAN / MONIQUE SAMUELS / ASHLEY DARBY / KAREN HUGER

"ANDY, ARE YOU HOSTING? ARE YOU GOING TO ASK ME THE QUESTIONS? BECAUSE THIS CHILD IS ALL OVER THE PLACE." —KAREN, ABOUT ASHLEY

Things were brought up at this reunion that continued to be brought up for many seasons to come: Karen's alleged relationship with "blue eyes," Ashley's merry-go-round relationship with her husband, and, of course, the women saying that Karen puts on airs.

AIRED

2017

SEASON 3

CAST MEMBERS

CANDIACE DILLARD BASSETT / MONIQUE SAMUELS / KAREN HUGER / GIZELLE BRYANT / ASHLEY DARBY / ROBYN DIXON

I THINK I was so engrossed with the ladies of season three that I FORGOT to take their pictures!!

AIRED

2018

This was CANDIACE'S first season and she quickly earned her spot in the group. She was SHARP with SHADE and proved she was NOT to be toyed with.

"I DON'T NEED TO BRING ANOTHER WOMAN ON THE SHOW TO RUFFLE YOUR FEATHERS. I CAN BREATHE AND DO THAT. ALL ON MY OWN!" —MONIQUE

SEASON 4

CAST MEMBERS

GIZELLE BRYANT /
CANDIACE DILLARD BASSETT /
ROBYN DIXON / MONIQUE SAMUELS /
KAREN HUGER / ASHLEY DARBY

"DO YOU WANT TO START WITH THE WIG OR END WITH THE WIG?" —ANDY

"I WANT THAT WIG TO BURN." —GIZELLE

I think KAREN and GIZELLE are two of the BEST FRENEMIES *The Real Housewives* has ever seen, as exemplified by the season three reunion.

AIRED

2019

The women wore WHITE—
and that added an ANGELIC
vibe to all the shade!

SEASON 5

CAST MEMBERS

GIZELLE BRYANT / CANDIACE DILLARD BASSETT / WENDY OSEFO / MONIQUE SAMUELS / ASHLEY DARBY / ROBYN DIXON / KAREN HUGER

"YOUR PASTOR BOYFRIEND IS SWINGING HIS BIG D ALL AROUND ATLANTA."—MONIQUE

This was our COVID reunion, in YELLOW.

"THE VOCALS, MY DEAR, ARE TRASH."—CANDIACE TO ASHLEY

AIRED

2020

We were socially distanced, as you can see, but that didn't stop Monique from delivering one of the most iconic receipts in reunion history—her binder. There was a moment when Monique was going in so hard on Gizelle that I felt terrible for her. But then I was also stunned and impressed by Gizelle's stoicism through Monique's sustained questioning.

SEASON 6

CAST MEMBERS

GIZELLE BRYANT / CANDIACE DILLARD BASSETT / ROBYN DIXON / ASHLEY DARBY / MIA THORNTON / KAREN HUGER / WENDY OSEFO

The women were tired, but when NICKI MINAJ walked on set, they all completely lit up with excitement.

This year was notable for two reasons; it was the first time I shared the reunion stage with another host—Nicki Minaj!—and it was the year that Gizelle's and Candiace's husbands' alleged interaction in Gizelle's hotel room ended their friendship and drove a lot of the drama the following season. But let's focus on Nicki's role because that's a happier story. She had been passionate about her fandom of *Potomac* and had tweeted that she would love to host the reunion. When I saw that, I immediately texted her publicist and said we would love to make her part of the show. She was incredibly passionate, eager, and kind to

People ask me if there are other CELEBRITIES I could see doing this, and two that come to mind are JENNIFER LAWRENCE and RIHANNA.

AIRED

2021

work with. Beforehand, I told her to make this her own experience; she could ask whatever she wanted and have fun with the women. We hid Nicki in a hotel room away from the wives and brought her out once we'd completed taping the main show, which was, by this point, at eight or nine P.M. I gleefully stepped aside and watched Nicki host her version of the reunion, with the rest of the producers in the back of the studio. She was going in on a few of the women in ways that I would never—and from the perspective not only of a fan but also, of another woman. I thought her point of view was really fresh and interesting. She asked questions I could never get away with in a million years!

SEASON 7

CAST MEMBERS

GIZELLE BRYANT / ASHLEY DARBY / WENDY OSEFO / MIA THORNTON / ROBYN DIXON / CANDIACE DILLARD BASSETT / KAREN HUGER

Things got really dark and contentious this year, especially between Candiace and Gizelle. A huge online conversation about colorism surrounded the show, a topic about which I did not feel qualified or comfortable moderating. We considered bringing someone else

"MICHELLE OBAMA IS WATCHING."—ANDY "SHE HAS TURNED THE CHANNEL."—CANDIACE

AIRED

2023

in to address these issues with the ladies but ultimately asked them how they would like to handle it, and they all said they would like to address it themselves on their own. So I sat and listened and learned. I was proud of them for their honest discourse and of me for keeping my mouth shut.

SEASON 8

CAST MEMBERS

KAREN HUGER / GIZELLE BRYANT / ROBYN DIXON / NNEKA IHIM / ASHLEY DARBY / WENDY OSEFO / CANDIACE DILLARD BASSETT / MIA THORNTON

On the tape day for this reunion, I was at a personal emotional low, having been, for twenty-four hours, the subject of a raft of negative press based on ridiculous, baseless claims. That's what made it absolutely incredible when Gizelle and Karen crowned me the "duke of Potomac." It's a title as meaningless as "the grande dame," but on that day you would have thought I had been crowned by the queen herself. It was really sweet of them. I felt taken care of by these women.

"YOU KNOW IN POTOMAC WE LIVE BY A CORONATION." —GIZELLE

AIRED

2024

SEASON 9

CAST MEMBERS

GIZELLE BRYANT / ASHLEY DARBY / KEIARNA STEWART / STACEY RUSCH / WENDY OSEFO / MIA THORNTON

This reunion is not only my favorite *Potomac* reunion but also the most fun I've had in a reunion in years for three reasons. First, the women were at their funniest. Second, Gizelle and Wendy had a rapport going throughout the day that was giving me Gizelle-Karen frenemy vibes. Third, the allegations relating to Stacey and TJ made

"LEAVE MAYA ANGELOU ALONE! LEAVE HER ALONE!"—GIZELLE

AIRED

2025

for a dramatic few hours, with us having a lot of laughs while we tried to get to the truth. This is the first reunion where I got up and sat on the couch with the women. It ended with Stacey quoting Maya Angelou. She was in the hot seat for many hours and did not break a sweat—the hallmark of a great housewife!

SEASON 10

CAST MEMBERS

STACEY RUSCH / ASHLEY DARBY / KEIARNA STEWART / ANGEL MASSIE / TIA GLOVER / GIZELLE BRYANT / WENDY OSEFO

We shot this reunion at a studio across from the CBS Broadcast Center, home of my first job in New York City. As Gizelle pointed out to me, it was also the spot where we shot the season one reunion. We had two housewives at different phases of their brushes with the law. The first was Wendy Osefo, who for years was a great housewife role model. Since her first episode, she led with her education, Nigerian pride, and love of her family, but now faced serious fraud charges. I knew she wasn't going to be

"FOLLOW ME HERE, PROFESSOR. SHUT THE FUCK UP."—KAREN TO WENDY

AIRED

2026

able to speak very much on the charges she was facing, but we both became very emotional when I pointed out what a role model she had been on the show for so many years. The second was Karen Huger, who joined us after having completed her sentence and her Barbara Walters–style post-release grilling from me months earlier. The juxtaposition between them was stark and sad. All the ladies were very happy to see Karen, but they seemed very uneasy and uncomfortable figuring out how to support Wendy.

EARLY BRAVO

Before I was on the air, I was a Bravo executive (who blogged!) in charge of programming and development, focusing a ton of time on developing new hits and making *Top Chef* and *Project Runway* as great as they could be. *Top Chef* was an especially fun and happy environment where deep friendships were formed during lots of intense late nights and great food, creating what has become an Emmy-winning game-changer in the world of food TV.

TOP CHEF

I took this photo of Gail asleep at the judges' table in the dead of night at the season two finale in Hawaii. It was an especially memorable trip for all of us—the locations were beautiful and we were wrapping up a dramatic season featuring an intense rivalry between Marcel Vigneron and Ilan Hall.

Here's PADMA and me on top of ASPEN Mountain, shooting the season three finale.

I love Padma in her CURLERS and Hawaiian top.

This is a blurry picture taken from video village at the *Top Chef* season one finale. While I loved the many hours I spent in video village for *Project Runway* and *Top Chef* watching deliberations and eliminations, it was also so laborious and time-consuming . . . to be honest, I don't miss it.

This picture of Gail, Tom, and Padma was taken on one of Padma's first days as the host of *Top Chef* on season two. I liked her immediately!

HEADSHOTS

This is a collection of EARLY headshots of mine.

Not sure what was happening with me and that KNIFE.

PROJECT RUNWAY

Project Runway was such an exciting show to be a part of—it was the template for many creative-driven competition shows to come and a huge part of the cultural zeitgeist. I was especially gratified when Sarah Jessica Parker, a fan of the show, came to guest-judge during season four.

In the early years of *Project Runway*, we would invite talent from other shows to the finale. Here's Countess Luann de Lesseps and Michael Kors.

Here is a young CHRISTIAN SIRIANO backstage before he won season four.

This is from a night out at the now closed, but very legendary, New York City nightlife diner Florent. Of this group, only Lauri and George remain married.

Here I am with the season two gang of the *The Real Housewives of Orange County* at a Bravo press event.

ANDY'S OFFICE

In the early years, Bravo talent would stop by my office and I would shoot interviews with them on a digital camera, which we would upload to BravoTV.com. How analog.

FLIPPING OUT

This was taken on the set of the first *Flipping Out* reunion. I can't believe how hairy my chest is. (And I don't know where all the hair went!) It was at this reunion that producer Michael Davies saw something in me that made him want to work with me. He then went to Bravo with the idea of using his small studio to transfer my BravoTV.com show, *Watch What Happens Live,* to an actual late-night show on Bravo itself.

Miami

MUCH like the show itself, *Miami* reunions have had a rocky ride. They were as fraught as the series itself, but I will say they are always really colorful and fun. The first three seasons can almost live as their own (canceled) series, which we resurrected years later after a lot of fan demand. The second iteration of *Miami* featured a great run of memorable reunion moments.

ISO 100 ▷3
ISO 100 ▷4

ISO 100 ▷3
ISO 100 ▷4

ISO 100
ISO 100
L!VE
mazel by Bravo
happens
L!VE
happens
L!VE
mazel Bravo
ISO 100 ▷3
ISO 100 ▷4

ISO 100
ISO 100
ISO 100 ▷3
ISO 100 ▷4

ISO 100
ISO 100
ISO 100 ▷3
ISO 100 ▷4

ISO 100
ISO 100
ISO 100 ▷3
ISO 100 ▷4

"IF YOU KEEP SPREADING YOUR LIES ABOUT ME, I'M GOING TO START SPREADING THE TRUTH ABOUT YOU." —LEA "PLEASE HELP. SINCERELY, MARYSOL'S LIVER." —ANDY, READING ADRIANA'S LETTER "I HAVE REAL JOBS. IT'S NOT LIKE YOU. PUTTING PEOPLE TO SLEEP." —LARSA TO DR. NICOLE (AN ANESTHESIOLOGIST) "THE BONER YOU HAVE FOR ME . . . YOU NEED TO GO TO THE BATHROOM AND SMACK ONE OUT, GIRLFRIEND." —NICOLE "I'M A VERY GOOD FRIEND, BUT I'M A VERY BAD ENEMY." —MAMA ELSA

"SHE WAS CHEATING ON MARTINA WITH A HAITIAN MORTICIAN!" —ADRIANA ABOUT JULIA "YOUR BUTT?" —ANDY "MY BOOBS." —LARSA "BUT YOUR BUTT?" —ANDY "NO." —LARSA, WHEN ASKED WHAT PLASTIC SURGERY SHE'S HAD DONE "IF EVERYONE DID WHAT I WAS DOING, THIS SHOW WOULD BE ROCKING RIGHT NOW. IF WE HAD SIX ADRIANAS ON THIS SHOW, THIS SHOW WOULD BE BIGGER THAN *BEVERLY HILLS*." —ADRIANA DE MOURA

SEASON 1

CAST MEMBERS

LARSA PIPPEN / CRISTY RICE / ALEXIA NEPOLA / ADRIANA DE MOURA / MARYSOL PATTON / LEA BLACK

This was the biggest DISASTER of any reunion we've ever done. Somehow, we came up with the (BAD) idea to produce the season one *Miami* reunion live in THE CLUBHOUSE.

The ratings had been soft, so we weren't in a place where we were going to commit to a full-blown reunion. We decided instead that perhaps the hook of it being live would be enough to draw in more viewers. It was terrible. Every reunion features the women talking all over one another—but editing allows us to use the clearest bits. This was just a free-for-all, like unleashing six wild animals and expecting them to calmly come to some resolution under

Interesting to note how completely different LARSA PIPPEN looks in these pictures.

MARYSOL looks like the BABY version of herself.

AIRED

2011

insane time pressure. The result was an unintelligible screaming fest. This reunion was living proof of why we would never do these shows live again, but also why it takes so long to film them. I spend a good chunk of filming days reprimanding the ladies for talking over one another and trying to get clear, uninterrupted points out of people, which was just impossible in that setting. I truly have terrible memories of that night. The feeling of losing control on live television is not pleasant.

SEASON 2

CAST MEMBERS

JOANNA KRUPA / LISA HOCHSTEIN / KARENT SIERRA / LEA BLACK / ANA QUINCOCES / MARYSOL PATTON / ADRIANA DE MOURA

"PEOPLE LOVE MIAMI, BUT THEY DON'T LOVE IT BECAUSE IT'S A FUN PLACE. THEY LOVE IT BECAUSE IT'S A VERY ODD PLACE." – MAMA ELSA

This season was the DEBUT of the absolutely shockingly BEAUTIFUL Joanna Krupa, who to this day, I would argue, is the single GREATEST-LOOKING housewife in the history of the franchise. To quote Tamra, "That's my OPINION!!"

AIRED

2012
2013

MAMA ELSA added a lot of levity and fun to the season two reunion.

SEASON 3

CAST MEMBERS

JOANNA KRUPA / LEA BLACK / MARYSOL PATTON / ALEXIA NEPOLA / ADRIANA DE MOURA / LISA HOCHSTEIN

The season three *Miami* reunion is truly when everything went off the rails for the show. It felt like a telenovela, but not in a fun way. It was so dark. The women were just nasty to one another. There was no resolution and unfortunately as that season progressed, the ratings went down, and in a chilling sign that marked the inevitable future of that franchise, the ratings went down *for the reunion* instead of

"WHY WOULD I WANT A MAN WITH A LIMP PENIS?"—ADRIANA

AIRED

2013

up, which is the only time I remember that happening in *Housewives* history. So the decision to shelve *Miami* after that reunion didn't feel surprising inside the walls of Bravo. Another crucial occurrence that to me represented the death of the series was Mama Elsa taking ill in the middle of the season. I feel strongly that she was the heart and soul of that show and without her, it was a bit rudderless.

SEASON 4

CAST MEMBERS

JULIA LEMIGOVA / ADRIANA DE MOURA / GUERDY ABRAIRA / NICOLE MARTIN / LISA HOCHSTEIN / LARSA PIPPEN / MARYSOL PATTON / ALEXIA NEPOLA

Through the years that *Miami* was off the air, I remained cordial with Adriana de Moura, Alexia Nepola, Marysol Patton, and Lea Black, who were always remarkably positive and even somewhat optimistic about the idea that *Miami* might someday come back. I was less optimistic, despite regular questions from the fans asking if it would ever return. But with the launch of NBC's streaming platform, Peacock, it

Miami reunions marked the ONLY ONES in franchise HISTORY that started with a TEQUILA SHOT at the BEGINNING of the tape day (around 10 A.M.).

AIRED

2022

struck us that bringing *Miami* back on the streamer was something that would be a real gift to the fans, and a reason for them to subscribe to Peacock. So eight years later, we brought it back with a mix of the old and new. The reunions that followed were some of my favorites. The women looked amazing and the arguments were simultaneously emotional and ridiculous, which in my mind is the backbone of great *Housewives* interactions at reunions.

SEASON 5

CAST MEMBERS

NICOLE MARTIN / JULIA LEMIGOVA / ADRIANA DE MOURA / GUERDY ABRAIRA / KIKI BARTH / MARYSOL PATTON / ALEXIA NEPOLA / LARSA PIPPEN / LISA HOCHSTEIN

Some of the women's OUTFITS are vaguely reminiscent of PRINCESS LEIA at the feet of JABBA THE HUTT. (Does that make *me* Jabba??)

This reunion was a doozy. Adriana, who is not known for her timing, decided after she and Marysol made up to hand me her prop, which turned out to be a letter from Marysol's liver to Marysol, begging her to stop drinking. It was so absurdly hilarious, made especially so by how poorly timed it was.

AIRED

2023

“REUNION DAY. WITH OUR *CHARLIE'S ANGELS* . . . WHAT'S HIS NAME?”—LISA
“CHARLIE.”—ANDY

SEASON 6

CAST MEMBERS

GUERDY ABRAIRA / ALEXIA NEPOLA / JULIA LEMIGOVA / KIKI BARTH / MARYSOL PATTON / ADRIANA DE MOURA / NICOLE MARTIN / LISA HOCHSTEIN / LARSA PIPPEN

"CAN TWO THINGS BE TRUE: CAN A WOMAN LOVE MARTINA

I loved this reunion, not only because it was wall-to-wall absurd drama (my favorite kind), and not just because Adriana wore a crown of roses, but also because it ended with Julia singing a disco version of "Ave Maria."

AIRED

2024

NAVRATILOVA AND LOVE BLACK PENISES?"—ANDY

SEASON 7

CAST MEMBERS

ALEXIA NEPOLA / LARSA PIPPEN / JULIA LEMIGOVA / MARYSOL PATTON / KIKI BARTH / ADRIANA DE MOURA / GUERDY ABRAIRA / LISA HOCHSTEIN / STEPHANIE SHOJAEE

I don't know how we'll ever top the insanity of this reunion, which was rocked when Julia admitted to a dalliance she had had years before with Adriana, who leveled some truth bombs at Julia in the form of a Haitian mortician and coffee maker. I think the other housewives and I were in an amused state of shock during the entire back-and-forth.

AIRED

2025

"WHY DID YOU HAVE TO BUY THE HAITIAN MORTICIAN A COFFEE MAKER?"—ANDY

New
Jersey

WHEN people ask me which reunions are the hardest to film, I always think of *Jersey* because the family dynamics became more intense and fraught as the series went on, making it harder to drive to any resolution and more impossible for me to be heard in the room. I have a headache just looking through all these reunion pictures. My frustration with this group also has to do with some of their inability to listen, own responsibility for things, and move forward. There are a lot of hardheaded people in the Garden State!

Real Housewives

“YOU ARE GARBAGE AND YOU ARE DISGRACEFUL!” –CAROLINE “DO NOT BRING UP MY FAMILY!” –TERESA “I’M IN A WHIRLWIND OF STUPID.”– CAROLINE “TERESA, WHEN WE DIE THE VIEWERS WILL NOT BE AT OUR FUNERALS.” –CAROLINE “YOU’RE THE DEVIL AGAIN CAUSE YOU’RE WEARING RED.” –TERESA “AND YOU’RE GREEN WITH ENVY.” –JACQUELINE LAURITA “YOU MESS WITH ME AND YOU GO RIGHT BACK TO JAIL. CLINK CLINK!” –KIM D. TO TERESA

"YOU COULDN'T GET A MAN LIKE JOE GORGA EVEN IF YOU WERE THE LAST WHORE IN AMERICA!" —MELISSA TO KIM D. "I LOSE BRAIN CELLS TALKING TO YOU." —JACKIE GOLDSCHNEIDER "MONEY CAN'T BUY YOU CLASS BUT IT CAN'T BUY YOU A PERSONALITY EITHER." —JENNIFER TO JACKIE GOLDSCHNEIDER "BITCH BOY . . . I'M SORRY, JOE. YOU'RE KIND OF LIKE A HOUSEWIFE. SORRY, YOU ARE." —TERESA "YOU WANTED THIS. YOU CAME ON THE SHOW BEHIND MY BACK!" —TERESA TO MELISSA

SEASON 1

CAST MEMBERS

DINA MANZO / JACQUELINE LAURITA / CAROLINE MANZO / TERESA GIUDICE / DANIELLE STAUB

The first *Jersey* reunion was just nuts! We shot it in what I'm told was a studio but felt like an abandoned warehouse near some train tracks somewhere in the middle of the state. It all felt very questionable, including one of the top two worst sets in *Housewives* history (see page 107 for the other). The women had not spoken to one another as a group since filming the table flip. Tensions were incredibly high, not to mention that Teresa and Jacqueline were both very pregnant.

The PARQUET FLOOR and CHANDELIERS with blue background gave it some sort of a SURREALIST Jersey NIGHTMARE VIBE—one that carried over to what was happening in the room.

AIRED

2009

I remember that there was some sort of a Manzo family secret that Caroline didn't want to discuss at the reunion, and she was in tears at one point, giving one of what would later become very classic Caroline Manzo soliloquies. This was the first time we ever used a split-screen technique in postproduction on a reunion show. It was also the reunion in which I publicly "came out" (for the two people who might've thought I was straight) during a discussion of a gay slur said by Joe Giudice.

SEASON 2

CAST MEMBERS

TERESA GIUDICE / JACQUELINE LAURITA / CAROLINE MANZO / DANIELLE STAUB

The season two reunion is notable for several reasons. It was the first of several reunions we shot at the Borgata Hotel Casino & Spa in Atlantic City. We all spent the night before filming in the casino and some stayed the night of (I hightailed it back to Manhattan). And of course, Danielle brought up being in touch with Teresa's sister-in-law and intimated that Teresa didn't visit her newborn nephew in the hospital, which caused Teresa to lose her mind and lunge at Danielle, who kind of slither-strutted off the stage. As I tried to hold Teresa back, she hurled me onto my chair like a rag doll. So

"YOU UNDERSTAND YOU JUST THREW ME OFF OF YOU LIKE . . . VERY STRONG! HERE'S THE THING, JUST DON'T CROSS ME. OKAY? JUST DON'T CROSS ME."—ANDY

AIRED

2010

DANIELLE STAUB wore the first and only TANK TOP ever at a reunion, perhaps to illustrate her dabbling in her Sapphic era.

much happened at that reunion that Teresa pushing me didn't even register with me as being particularly notable. But as I was having a late nightcap with Mark Consuelos and Kelly Ripa that night in New York City, I said, "I think Teresa pushed me today." It was all such a blur. Later that summer when the reunion aired, that push, first seen in the super tease for the reunion, became so talked about that it went viral before going viral was even a thing. It was one of the moments in the early days that made people remember who I am. So I guess I have Teresa to thank for helping me climb a couple of notches on the ladder of fame.

SEASON 3

CAST MEMBERS

CAROLINE MANZO / MELISSA GORGA / KATHY WAKILE / TERESA GIUDICE

The season three reunion was a disaster entirely of our own making. Because the show was doing so well, we decided to film season three and season four back-to-back. So we were filming season four while season three was airing, which was incredibly complicated for a variety of reasons. But mainly, the women were not only reacting to what was happening to them in their lives as it was happening, but they were also reacting to the shows that were airing and the things that were being said about them. It was a mess. The confusion reached an apex when we were filming the season three reunion the day after a monumental fight occurred while shooting season four (that fight would become known as "Strippergate"). Tensions were so high that Jacqueline refused to show up at the season three reunion, which only later became a fireable offense. But at

"I'M LIKE LOOKING AT THE EXORCIST RIGHT NOW!"—TERESA TO CAROLINE

AIRED

2011

We shot this reunion on the STAGE at the Count Basie Theatre in Red Bank, New Jersey.

that point, we were already deep in production on a whole other season that included Jacqueline, so that punishment wasn't feasible. The morning was devoted to trying to get Jacqueline to return production's calls. When that failed, they went to her house but she wouldn't answer her front door. I'll never forget the chilling moment Caroline Manzo came into my dressing room and sat me down to tell it to me straight. "Jacqueline isn't coming, no matter what, and you should give up." Those weren't the exact words she used, but the message was clear. We started rolling soon after without Jacqueline. Explaining to the viewers why Jacqueline wasn't there was challenging, but I think weirdly, in the rearview mirror, it wound up being great promotion for the following season. The *Jersey* train ran like that for a few more years, with lots of recurring family mysteries and intrigue.

SEASON 4

CAST MEMBERS

TERESA GIUDICE / MELISSA GORGA / KATHY WAKILE / CAROLINE MANZO / JACQUELINE LAURITA

"SHE BETTER WATCH HER FUCKING TONGUE CAUSE I'LL CUT IT RIGHT THE FUCK OUT." —ROSIE (SCREAMING FROM BACKSTAGE)

I remember catching CAROLINE MANZO'S EYES several times, as we kind of silently chuckled to each other at the RIDICULOUSNESS of what was happening around us.

AIRED

2012

There were some laugh-out-loud moments of *Jersey*-style shade during the season four reunion, filmed again at the Borgata. Caroline Manzo had an ability to appreciate the absurdity of the *Jersey* drama, and that was a relationship that Caroline and I shared for years to come. That was the reunion that memorably featured Lauren Manzo daring Teresa to spell "napalm," Rosie screaming from backstage like a caged animal, and Joe Gorga and Giudice almost coming to blows. I had an insane amount of tanning makeup on (when in Rome!).

SEASON 5

CAST MEMBERS

MELISSA GORGA / KATHY WAKILE / CAROLINE MANZO / JACQUELINE LAURITA / TERESA GIUDICE

This reunion represented a fork in the road for this beloved franchise. Teresa's future was in question because of Joe's legal troubles, and it was Caroline Manzo's last as a housewife. While it broke my heart to see her go, she had clearly emotionally outgrown the show.

AIRED

2013

SEASON 6

CAST MEMBERS

DINA MANZO / NICOLE NAPOLITANO / TERESA APREA / AMBER MARCHESE / MELISSA GORGA / TERESA GIUDICE

The season six reunion represented the culmination of what I regard as the worst season in *Jersey* history. Our hope was that with a predominantly new cast, the show would be strong enough to continue while Teresa served her time. However, the addition of Amber and the twins Teresa Aprea and Nicole didn't resonate with the viewers in the way we'd hoped, and Dina Manzo had no interest in continuing on the show. This was a big part of the reason we decided

I will never forget talking to TERESA Giudice at the end of that day about her UNCERTAIN FUTURE as we wrapped filming. And I remember holding hands with her and really wondering if we would ever be on TELEVISION together again.

AIRED

2014

"I WISH I KNOW NOW WHAT I KNOW BACK THEN." –TERESA GIUDICE

to go on pause and wait for Teresa Giudice to get out of prison. But there was also the question of whether Teresa would come back to the show at all. There was a lot hanging in the balance. As we spoke, I felt sad for her that she would have to leave us. *Jersey* fans are so passionate and there had been a narrative among them that I didn't care for Teresa Giudice, which couldn't have been further from the truth. I think that moment showed people how I really felt.

SEASON 7

CAST MEMBERS

JACQUELINE LAURITA / SIGGY FLICKER / DOLORES CATANIA / MELISSA GORGA / TERESA GIUDICE

JACQUELINE was BACK, and Dolores joined the show!

This was Teresa's RETURN to the series after serving time, having left PRISON in great emotional and mental shape.

Most notably, Teresa Giudice accused Jacqueline and Caroline of having turned her in to the FBI.

AIRED

2016

“YOU GUYS SET ME UP! CALLING THE GOVERNMENT.” —TERESA

SEASON 8

CAST MEMBERS

MELISSA GORGA / SIGGY FLICKER / DOLORES CATANIA / DANIELLE STAUB / MARGARET JOSEPHS / TERESA GIUDICE

All these WOMEN have to do is SHOW UP to LIGHT the room up.

There were some stellar ONE-LINERS from Siggy and Margaret at this reunion . . .

. . . and relatively HILARIOUS CAMEOS from Kim DePaola and DANIELLE STAUB.

AIRED

2018

"DON'T TALK ABOUT MY FOYER AND I WON'T TALK ABOUT YOURS."—SIGGY FLICKER

SEASON 9

CAST MEMBERS

TERESA GIUDICE / DOLORES CATANIA / JENNIFER AYDIN / JACKIE GOLDSCHNEIDER / MELISSA GORGA / MARGARET JOSEPHS

"YOU LIKE BIG DICKS? I GOT ONE TOO." —JENNIFER

"Are you kidding me? This is for my GUY!" —ANDY, when he saw the toy car the women gifted him for his soon-to-be-born son, BEN

Jen Aydin and Jackie Goldschneider were excellent additions to the cast this year. There was drama everywhere and it felt like we had a cast that was going to serve us for years to come. If *SNL* did a *Jersey* reunion parody, I think the women gave them plenty of hair and costume inspiration!

AIRED

2019

"I LOSE BRAIN CELLS TALKING TO YOU." —JACKIE GOLDSCHNEIDER

SEASON 10

CAST MEMBERS

MARGARET JOSEPHS / MELISSA GORGA / JACKIE GOLDSCHNEIDER / JENNIFER AYDIN / DOLORES CATANIA / TERESA GIUDICE

This was Danielle Staub's last season. She was still a friend, and she had all sorts of demands about where she was going to sit. She wanted to sit next to me. (Housewives either *really* want to sit next to me or really do *not*. For some it's

"YOU ALL JUDGE ME." —JENNIFER

"NOT BY YOUR COVER. YOUR COVER IS GORGEOUS. IT'S THE INSIDES THAT SUCK."—MARGARET

AIRED

2020

cachet, yet others realize it means they're in the hot seat.) But we wanted her on the end of the couch. After a lot of circular conversations, she wound up sitting in a chair off to the side. I don't think she was happy about it.

SEASON 11

CAST MEMBERS

TERESA GIUDICE / DOLORES CATANIA / JENNIFER AYDIN / JACKIE GOLDSCHNEIDER / MELISSA GORGA / MARGARET JOSEPHS

“I GOT A NEW VAGINA.”—DOLORES

AIRED

2021

Somehow for this COVID reunion, I didn’t take a picture of the ladies on my right. I can’t find it anywhere! But there is a picture of Melissa, Jackie, and Margaret FaceTiming with Ben.

“TERESA, I’M LOOKING AT THOSE LIPS . . . I FEEL LIKE THEY’RE A LITTLE BIGGER THAN THE LAST TIME I SAW YOU.”—ANDY

SEASON 12

CAST MEMBERS

MARGARET JOSEPHS / JACKIE GOLDSCHNEIDER / MELISSA GORGA / DOLORES CATANIA / JENNIFER AYDIN / TERESA GIUDICE

A few *Jersey* reunions over the years were unsuccessful at providing any resolution and, in fact, wound up making the women's relationships with one another even worse—season twelve being one of them. This reunion also featured me absolutely losing my mind as I failed to not only handhold the ladies to any resolution but also to simply get a word in edgewise.

“AM I THE ONLY ONE WITH SENSE IN THIS WHOLE FUCKING ROOM?”—MELISSA

AIRED

2022

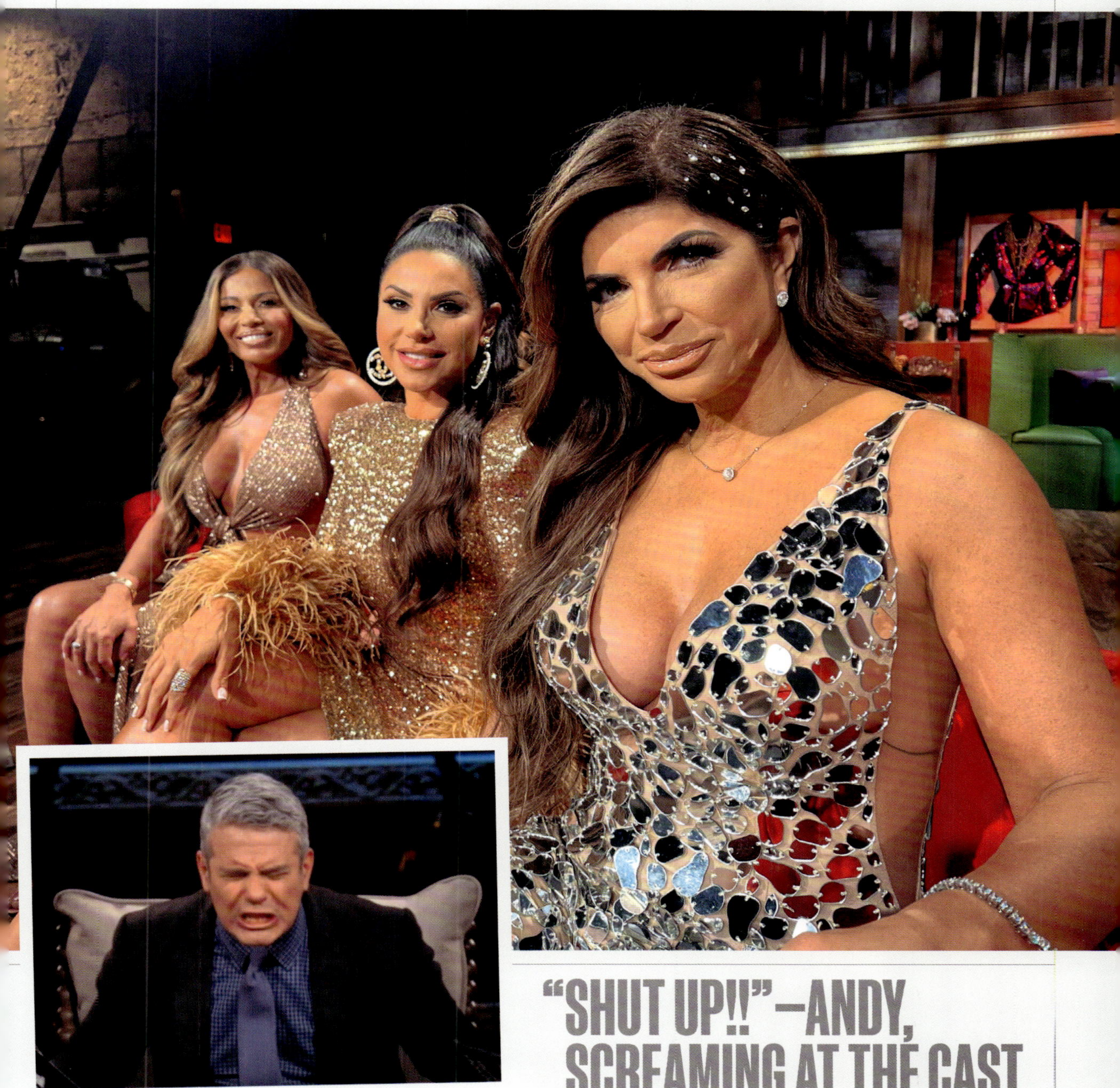

“SHUT UP!!”—ANDY, SCREAMING AT THE CAST

SEASON 13

CAST MEMBERS

TERESA GIUDICE / JENNIFER AYDIN / DOLORES CANTANIA / DANIELLE CABRAL / RACHEL FUDA / MARGARET JOSEPHS / MELISSA GORGA

This was the official dead-end reunion. Old, old, old problems festering, combined with a group-wide inability to give an inch. It is no surprise that this would represent the last formal reunion we did with this cast. The next season we took one last chance with them (with

"I'M NEVER GOING TO LOOK AT YOUR FACE AGAIN."—TERESA TO MELISSA

AIRED

2023

team Melissa vs. team Teresa) and suffice it to say, they stayed in their corners the entire season. They were so dug in, we didn't even bother filming a reunion. We just didn't see a point. Instead, we gathered the women in two separate rooms at Rails Steakhouse to gab about the season.

Atlanta

HANDS down some of my best reunion moments have taken place at Atlanta's Biltmore Hotel, where we shot the bulk of the early reunions. *The Real Housewives of Atlanta* has created a rushing river of reunion GIFs and memorable lines that are quoted today with the same glee as they were when they first aired. After season one of *Atlanta*, Bravo wasn't yet at a point where we were sure if we would do a reunion after every season of every series, though I'd hosted one for *Orange County* and one for *New York*'s inaugural season. I remember Nene Leakes calling me in the office to advocate for us coming down to Atlanta and shooting a reunion. She said she had so much she felt she needed to say to Kim, now that the show was airing. Little did I know that "Close your legs to married men" was at the top of her to-do list for Miss Zolciak. And we were off and running.

“CLOSE YOUR LEGS TO MARRIED MEN.” —NENE “I LIKE THE BEAT.” —SHEREÉ “FIX THAT BODY!” —NENE “FIX THAT FACE!” —SHEREÉ “BECAUSE YOU’RE SELLING A BOOTY MADE IN MEXICO.” —PHAEDRA “I SAID WHAT I SAID!” —NENE “NOW WHY AM I IN IT? SEE HOW I GET THROWN INTO STUFF. I AIN’T EVEN DID NOTHIN’.” —NENE “ON YOUR BEST DAY AND MY WORST, YOU WOULDN’T EVEN BE THIRD RUNNER-UP.” —KENYA TO PHAEDRA “THE LIES! THE LIES! THE LIES!” —KANDI

"JOGGERS." —SHEREÉ
"WHERE IS YOUR SCOOTER? WHERE IS IT?" —NENE TO KIM
"I CAN'T BE BOUGHT, KANDI. I'M NOT GONNA BE BOUGHT INTO NOT SPEAKING UP TO YOUR ASS." —PORSHA TO KANDI
"FIX IT, JESUS." — PHAEDRA
"MY BOOTY? BITCH, YOU CRAZY, THIS IS ALL NATURAL, HONEY. SQUATS NOT SHOTS, HONEY." —SHEREÉ
"WATCH, BITCH!" —KIM "YOU TOUCH ME, GIRL, I WILL WHACK THAT WIG OFF YOUR HEAD!" —NENE

SEASON 1

CAST MEMBERS

SHEREÉ WHITFIELD / KIM ZOLCIAK / NENE LEAKES / LISA WU / DESHAWN SNOW

The women look like they're DRESSED to go to LUNCH at a department store, don't they?

"SO YOU DIDN'T HAVE CANCER?"—ANDY "NO I DID NOT."—KIM

AIRED

2008

This was the first time we shot at the Atlanta Biltmore Hotel and Tower. Whatever furniture we had for the set was not working, so the two leather couches you see in that reunion were actually ones executive producer Steven Weinstock and I found in the lobby. He and I and a few other guys carried those couches into one of the grand ballrooms and said, "Well, these look good enough." For years to come, I would go to that hotel and see those inconspicuous leather couches in the lobby and think about how no one realized what an important part of TV history they were. Maybe we should add a plaque one day to commemorate them.

When Nene was firing off one-liners at Kim, it was the first time at a reunion I felt that I didn't have control of the room. The emotion was just *happening.* I didn't realize just how funny the entire show was going to play out on television. The exchange that most resonated with me was the circuitous conversation that Kim and I had about her cancer journey, which I knew at the time (Chili's parking lot?) would be talked about by our viewers. I was also stunned when Kim told me she was thirty years old! And that was also the day Nene Leakes gave me the nickname "Buttercup," which stuck for years to come. I think our special bond started on that day.

SEASON 2

CAST MEMBERS

NENE LEAKES / LISA WU /
SHEREÉ WHITFIELD / KANDI BURRUSS /
KIM ZOLCIAK

We filmed the season two reunion at a CLUB and it featured a LIVE performance by Kim Zolciak with "TARDY FOR THE PARTY," which landed like a thud among the other women and elicited great SHADE from Shereé . . .

AIRED
2009

SEASON 3

CAST MEMBERS

NENE LEAKES / CYNTHIA BAILEY / SHEREÉ WHITFIELD / PHAEDRA PARKS / KANDI BURRUSS / KIM ZOLCIAK

During the season three reunion, Phaedra's and Cynthia's first, there was a massive, rare ice storm in Atlanta that shut down the airport. Executive producer Steven Weinstock and I had to take a private plane to Birmingham, Alabama, and stay at a

"CAN'T GET MORE WOMAN THAN THIS."—SHEREÉ

We filmed the reunion in an AQUARIUM, which, needless to say, was very ODD.

AIRED

2011

PHAEDRA'S Hervé Léger dress was so constraining, she almost passed out.

Holiday Inn (or something like that) and then drive very slowly the next morning to Atlanta. There were a lot of questions about whether we would even be able to tape given the weather. It was probably the quietest Nene ever was at a reunion; her vibe matched what was happening outside.

SEASON 4

CAST MEMBERS

NENE LEAKES / CYNTHIA BAILEY / KANDI BURRUSS / PHAEDRA PARKS / SHEREÉ WHITFIELD / KIM ZOLCIAK

"NEVERLAND."—NENE, ABOUT CHATEAU SHEREÉ

TOPICS ranged from Kroy Biermann's BOOTY . . .

. . . to the progress of Chateau Shereé and Nene's TRUMP CHECKS. Which all in the rearview mirror feel like inconsensequal things to be disagreeing over, my FAVORITE kind!

AIRED

2012

This was SHEREÉ'S last reunion for some time. She would come and go over the next few years.

SEASON 5

CAST MEMBERS

NENE LEAKES / CYNTHIA BAILEY / PHAEDRA PARKS / PORSHA WILLIAMS / KANDI BURRUSS / KENYA MOORE

Season five was Porsha Williams's first reunion and, I thought, her last. I can't recall now why I was so sure we weren't going to pick her up, but what I will say is that she absolutely proved herself, not only as a human being, but as a great housewife that

"IN THE WORDS OF WHITNEY HOUSTON, SHOW ME THE RECEIPTS . . . GO ON, HONEY. TWIRL ON THAT!"—PHAEDRA, ABOUT KENYA'S WORKOUT VIDEO REVIEWS AND SALES

AIRED

2013

day, ending with an a cappella performance of "Amazing Grace." By wrap, I had become a fully indoctrinated fan of Porsha, which I remain to this day. I also remember an uneasy hug between Kim and Nene. And some hilarious debate about warring fitness videos.

SEASON 6

CAST MEMBERS

NENE LEAKES / KANDI BURRUSS / PHAEDRA PARKS / PORSHA WILLIAMS / CYNTHIA BAILEY / KENYA MOORE

One of my big reunion regrets was my lack of foresight about how poorly Kenya's bullhorn would go down. That incident was one of the low points of the series.

"YOU'RE A SLUT FROM THE '90S." —PORSHA TO KENYA

AIRED

2014

SEASON 7

CAST MEMBERS

NENE LEAKES / PHAEDRA PARKS / PORSHA WILLIAMS / CLAUDIA JORDAN / CYNTHIA BAILEY / KANDI BURRUSS / KENYA MOORE

FASHION-WISE, this was my FAVORITE *Atlanta* reunion! It was the first time we asked the women to COLOR COORDINATE.

The reads were on point, resulting in memes that are still everywhere! Nene's career outside the show was really blowing up with her roles on Broadway and her recurring part on *Glee,* so her relationship to being a housewife started to evolve. It was becoming a real possibility that she would not always be a part of the show and, in fact, outgrow us.

AIRED

2015

SEASON 8

CAST MEMBERS

PORSHA WILLIAMS / PHAEDRA PARKS / KIM FIELDS / SHEREÉ WHITFIELD / KANDI BURRUSS / CYNTHIA BAILEY / KENYA MOORE

After a lackluster season, KIM FIELDS really got the assignment at this reunion. In stark contrast to her appearance throughout the season, "Reunion Kim" was activated! I hoped when we left that there could be a way forward for her on the show. Alas, she decided not to come back.

TENS across the board for the CLOTHES for the rest of the ladies . . .

AIRED

2016

"SHE'S THE PRESIDENT OF THE FLIP-FLOP COMMITTEE." —PORSHA TO CYNTHIA

SEASON 9

CAST MEMBERS

PHAEDRA PARKS / PORSHA WILLIAMS / SHEREÉ WHITFIELD / CYNTHIA BAILEY / KENYA MOORE / KANDI BURRUSS

The season nine reunion was probably the most dramatic in *Atlanta* history, with the climactic reveal to the question asked all season long: "Who said that?" As it turns out, the answer was Phaedra. We shot until well after midnight with incredible, real-time behind-the-scenes drama that pushed us to our first-ever four-part reunion (we had

"PHAEDRA, WHY WOULDN'T YOU ADMIT YOU JUST STARTED THE RUMOR?"—ANDY

AIRED 2017

I absolutely loved CYNTHIA'S homage to MISS ROSS.

another the year I grilled Erika Jayne on *BH*). I was surprised at the time that Phaedra wasn't able to reingratiate herself with the women. I remember giving her several opportunities to apologize or explain herself, but nothing was landing. I hated seeing her leave the show, as she always made me smile. I also hated seeing Kandi so upset.

SEASON 10

CAST MEMBERS

NENE LEAKES / KANDI BURRUSS / SHEREÉ WHITFIELD / KENYA MOORE / CYNTHIA BAILEY / PORSHA WILLIAMS

"WHEN?"—ANDY

"UH PROBABLY, MORE SEPTEMBER. OR UH, THAT IS, UH, SPRING / SUMMER." —SHEREÉ

She by Shereé remains one of my favorite *Housewives* topics. At this reunion, I brought it up rather flippantly; it was something I always brought up to Shereé even years after she hadn't introduced it. My random question elicited one of the most memorable back-and-forths in reunion history. We finally got those joggers many years later.

AIRED

2018

SEASON 11

CAST MEMBERS

NENE LEAKES / KANDI BURRUSS / SHAMARI DEVOE / EVA MARCILLE / CYNTHIA BAILEY / PORSHA WILLIAMS

My predominant memory from this reunion was how miserable Nene was all day. She didn't seem to want to be there and her disdain for most of the other women permeated the room. She kept saying she wasn't friends with anyone on the couches, which of course negates the whole premise of the show. I love reunion-Nene but this was a tough one for her.

AIRED

2019

SEASON 12

CAST MEMBERS

KENYA MOORE / NENE LEAKES /
KANDI BURRUSS / PORSHA WILLIAMS /
EVA MARCILLE / CYNTHIA BAILEY

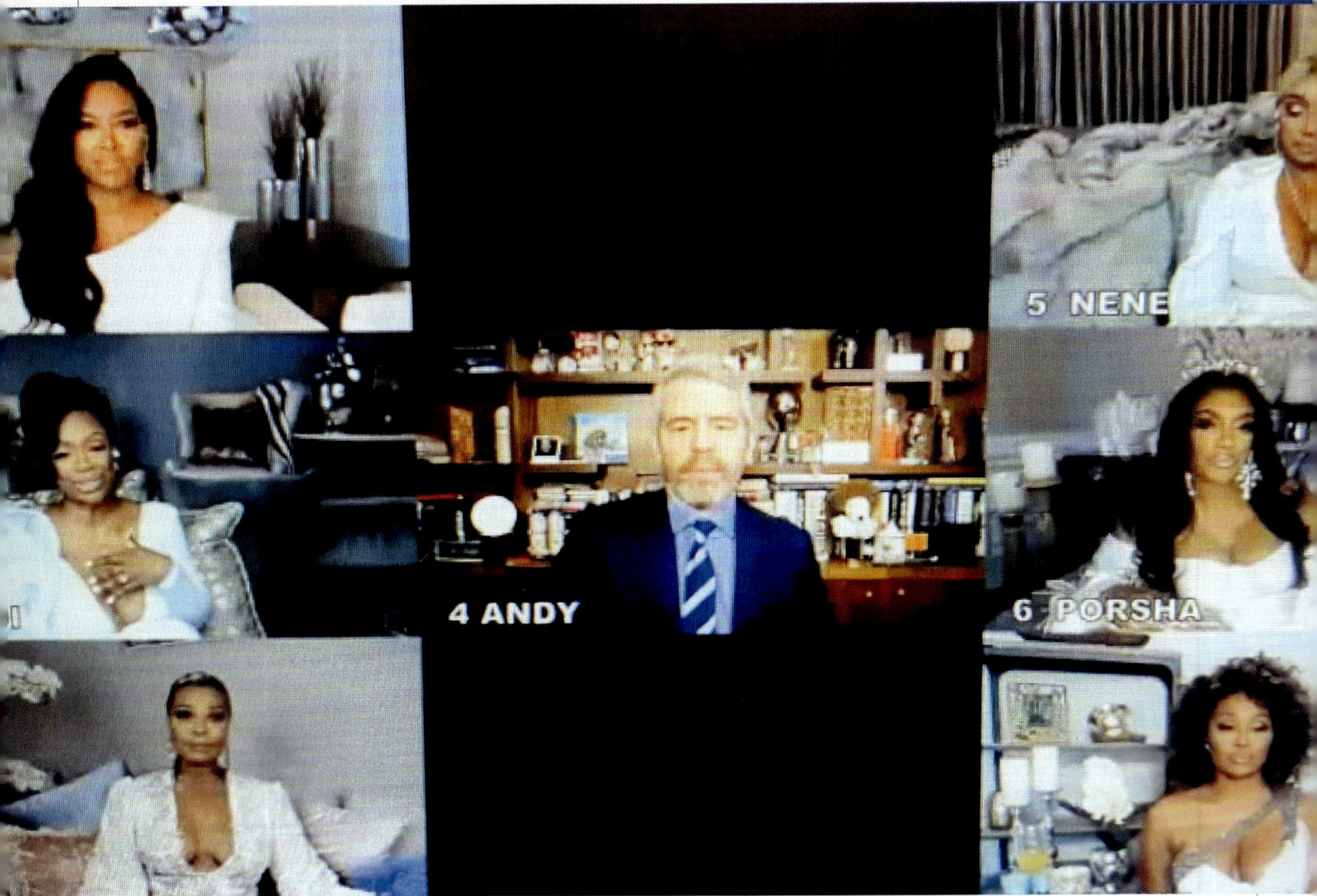

"YOU ARE NOT A SPRING CHICKEN, BOO BOO!"—PORSHA
"YOU ARE AN AGED HEN!"—EVA
"GIRL, THEM TITTIES IS AGED HENS! THEY SOCIAL DISTANCING. BITCH, DON'T COME FOR ME!"—PORSHA

"YOU WERE LICKING BOTTOMS TO STAY ON TOP!"—NENE TO EVA

AIRED

2020

These are PICTURES I took of my COMPUTER screen for our first-ever VIRTUAL REUNION, which became the norm as COVID continued to isolate the world.

You can see Nene's closed computer screen after she "walked off" (it's hard to walk off an at-home reunion because you're already . . . home, but her shutting her screen was pretty dramatic). This was a really frustrating reunion for me. It was hard to lead the conversation in a virtual setting and I knew that in a format geared toward resolution, we were hitting brick walls.

SEASON 13

CAST MEMBERS

PORSHA WILLIAMS / DREW SIDORA / KANDI BURRUSS / CYNTHIA BAILEY / KENYA MOORE

This was our socially distanced, dungeon-themed reunion, featuring boundary-pushing looks that, out of context of the season, would appear insane. Much of it was spent dissecting what did or didn't happen with Bolo. After a long run of iconic and fun reunions, this one felt like it belonged in a dungeon.

AIRED

2021

SEASON 14

CAST MEMBERS

SHEREÉ WHITFIELD / KENYA MOORE / KANDI BURRUSS / SANYA RICHARDS-ROSS / DREW SIDORA / MARLO HAMPTON

This reunion RESONATED for me on two fronts. ONE, I loved having Shereé back on the couch . . .

TWO, I was HAPPY that MARLO opened up so deeply about her life in foster care; her backstory made me understand her as a person.

AIRED

2022

SEASON 15

CAST MEMBERS

SHEREÉ WHITFIELD / MARLO HAMPTON / SANYA RICHARDS-ROSS / KANDI BURRUSS / KENYA MOORE / DREW SIDORA

Shereé's "SHE NEWS" prop had me in STITCHES! I still have it, and I will always have a SPECIAL PLACE in my heart for Shereé.

AIRED

2023

SEASON 16

CAST MEMBERS

SHAMEA MORTON MWANGI / ANGELA OAKLEY / KELLI FERRELL / DREW SIDORA / CYNTHIA BAILEY / PHAEDRA PARKS / PORSHA WILLIAMS

We were back in Atlanta to shoot the season sixteen reunion and as a producer, I felt like the show was better set for the future than it had been in previous seasons, with the addition of Angela, Kelli, and Shamea.

AIRED

2025

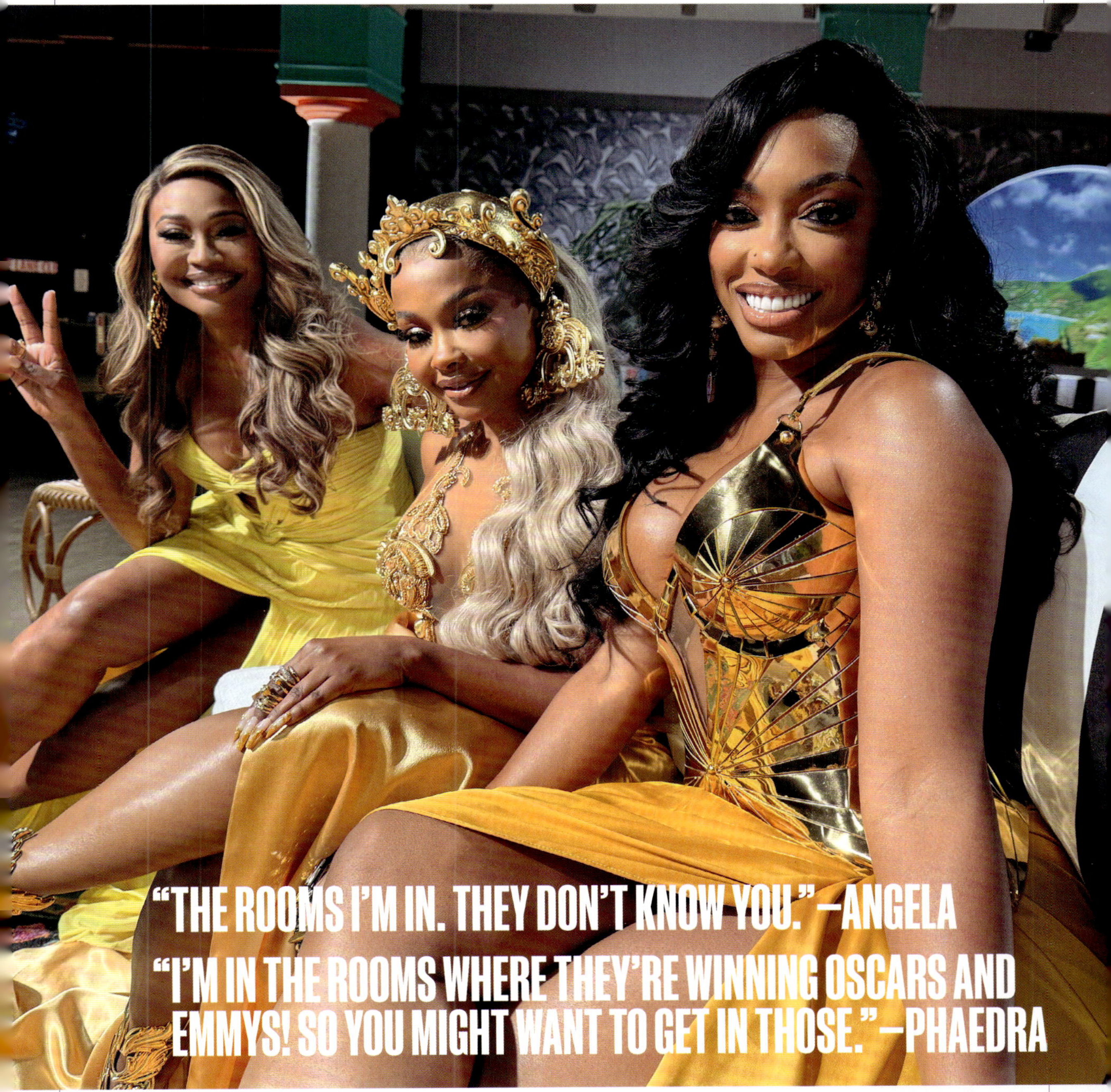

WWHL BTS

This is the first-ever episode of *Watch What Happens Live* featuring Danielle Staub drinking sweet white wine with a straw, again, and wearing her white tank top with kind of a nod to a flamenco dress. I don't remember a lot about that episode, except that I sweat a lot because we hadn't figured out the ventilation and that otherwise I wasn't nervous, just excited.

This was the first of many (at least one hundred?) appearances by the *Vanderpump Rules* gang. I can't believe how young and beautiful they are.

This is a picture I took of Nene Leakes on my BlackBerry before the nearly ten-minute-long fight she had with Kim Zolciak on the phone from the Bahamas in which she repeated the lines "trash box," "go to bed," and "close your legs to married men" on a loop. I have to say I didn't realize at the time how iconic that fight would become. And also a shout-out to Nene, who always brought a great time to The Clubhouse. Those were some of my favorite episodes.

After Slade Smiley accused Vicki Gunvalson of looking like Miss Piggy, how shady were we to bring the Muppet on to surprise Vicki? She took it like a champ.

We've showcased countless plastic surgery transformations on the show, and here I am backstage with Alexis Bellino before revealing either her new face or nose, I can't remember.

While I waited for Ben's birth in the hospital in L.A., my beloved *WWHL* staff sent me this pic to show they were waiting too . . . and I burst into tears. I love this picture and my team.

This was our New Year's Eve show counting down to 2011 with an insane group of people, including Nene, Lisa Vanderpump, Dina Manzo, and Meghan McCain. We "married" Dina's hairless cat Grandma Wrinkles to Giggy Vanderpump, did a wig drop at midnight, and Tamra and I made out as Kim performed "Tardy for the Party." The wig was styled by Derek J, and it was not his best work, to be kind. I remember we had to keep Kim Zolciak and Nene apart, while at the same time Nene and Vanderpump were at each other about whose show was more successful. Also, I've never been more hungover in my life than I was that day. I had "DJed" the night before at a club called Bedlam, which also described my scrambled brain. Between my hangover and the chaotic group of guests, I felt like I was landing a tin can in a hurricane. We never did a live New Year's show again.

This was the night we reunited Nene and Kim. We went out to TAO after and laughed late into the night.

I was excited to have Bethenny and Jeff Lewis on in 2022. Both were long off Bravo, but I considered them friends and masters of the genre of trash talking. Unfortunately, I think that episode resulted in the beginning of the end of my personal and professional relationship with Bethenny. Worth noting that while we were doing the episode, I thought it was going great and that she was, as usual, on top of her game. It was very clear after that night that she can dish it, but she can't take it.

This was one of my birthday shows and the staff had Melania, of whom I was a fan, walk out a "unicorn" to "gift" me for my birthday. It was all so camp and weird and wonderful. I still marvel at the number of housewives' kids I've watched grow into wonderful adults, and now that I'm a parent, it's put into perspective for me how quickly kids grow up.

WOMEN OF SNL

One of the highlights of my career occurred in 2010 when I was asked to play myself in a sketch featuring a murderer's row of SNL greats parodying our *Real Housewives* reunions, which took place in 30 Rock's famed Studio 8H on a set that mirrored our (god-awful) season one *RHONJ* acid trip of a set. I've been inspired and amazed by SNL's female ensemble members since the earliest days of their show, and being able to sit among them (as myself!) as they parodied our show was divine, surreal, and next to impossible to get through with a straight face. I am so glad that I grabbed my digital camera and took pics of the legends on either side of me before we shot!

ANA GASTEYER / RACHEL DRATCH / CHERI OTERI / KRISTEN WIIG / MOLLY SHANNON / MAYA RUDOLPH / TINA FEY / NORA DUNN

"YOU PULLED MY WEAVE, OKAY? YOU KNOW IT, ANDY KNOWS IT, AND THE WEAVE KNOWS IT!" —KRISTEN WIIG

New York City

RHONY reunions are up there with *Atlanta* as the most personally enjoyable and hilarious. The *RHONY* cast stood alone for years in that they tended to all go out to dinner together after taping, which really says something. I have so many memories of wrapping and then texting producers Jen O'Connell, Lisa Shannon, and Christian Barcellos the funny things the women had said throughout filming. For the years Bethenny was on, she and I always had a debrief after the reunion that would result in us dissolving into a puddle of laughter over the absolute insanity and ridiculousness of what we had filmed. *RHONY* holds a very special place in my heart.

"I DON'T LIKE WOMEN WHO TALK BEHIND MY BACK BECAUSE THAT'S NOT THE PRINCESSES I KNOW."—**LUANN**
"IF YOU WANNA SAY GREY GARDENS I LOVE THAT BECAUSE YOU KNOW WHAT? EDIE BEALE AND YOU KNOW HER MOM? THEY WERE CHARMING, TALENTED, SENSITIVE . . ."—**SONJA**
"THEY WERE MENTALLY ILL!"—**LUANN**
"OPINIONS ARE LIKE ASSHOLES. WE ALL HAVE THEM."—**BETHENNY**
"WELL GOOD. THEN THAT'S AN ASSHOLE OPINION."—**DORINDA** "BUT I HAVE A HUGE VAGINA."—**SONJA**

"YOU'RE AFRAID OF HER TOO, ANDY?" —CAROLE "DON'T TALK TO ME, MISS PINOT GRIGIO!" —LUANN TO RAMONA "GO WITH YOUR LOSER FRIENDS WHO ARE A PSA STATEMENT FOR A BAD FACELIFT. LIKE YOURS." —DORINDA TO RAMONA "*COSMOPOLITAN* RATED ME THE FIVE MOST NICE CELEBRITY EVER." —KELLY "YOU'RE NOT INSULAR. YOU'RE AT EVERY SINGLE PARTY THERE IS." —BETHENNY TO KELLY "JUST BECAUSE YOU SAY IT DOESN'T MAKE IT TRUE." —JILL

SEASON 1

CAST MEMBERS

ALEX MCCORD / JILL ZARIN / LUANN DE LESSEPS / RAMONA SINGER / BETHENNY FRANKEL

We shot the first reunion on LOCATION at the RUSSIAN TEA ROOM, where I had just had my fortieth birthday party, so I was really FAMILIAR with the space.

AIRED

2008

"YOU DON'T KNOW IF YOU'RE GONNA GET RAMONA OR REMEANA." —JILL

FUN FACTS: This was the first reunion where I sat in the middle of the housewives, and it was only the third reunion ever! It featured Ramona walking off set (the first reunion walk-off ever), Jill Zarin wearing a "Team Jill" shirt (the first time a housewife sold her own merch on the show), the first time a husband (Simon van Kempen) joined us, and Alex McCord defending her (tame) nude photos. The subject of Alex's photos is what spurred Ramona's walk-off. My recollection is that Ramona's daughter went to a private school and Ramona was worried that the association with naked pictures would somehow affect her daughter's standing at the school.

SEASON 2

CAST MEMBERS

KELLY BENSIMON / LUANN DE LESSEPS / RAMONA SINGER / JILL ZARIN / BETHENNY FRANKEL / ALEX MCCORD

AIRED

2009

This was an early preview for what would become my yearslong quest to get a roomful of housewives to speak one at a time and not interrupt one another. (The struggle continues twenty years later, in every city!) The Count and Luann had just split up. There was a lot of Brooklyn-shaming from Ramona, and Bethenny and Kelly were going at it in a very funny way, mainly over Bethenny calling Kelly "Madonna."

VINTAGE cameras produce DARK images!!

We shot season two at CIPRIANI Wall Street. The audio is really ECHOEY because it's a party space and the CEILINGS are REALLY HIGH.

"I MEAN YOU'RE NOT IN IRAQ COVERING THE WAR. I MEAN YOU'RE WRITING ABOUT, YOU KNOW, PAISLEY ZAC POSEN DRESSES. I MEAN IT'S LIKE GET A GRIP. REALLY." —BETHENNY TO KELLY "I JUST WANT TO ASK ONE QUESTION. DO YOU HAVE A LOT OF GIRLFRIENDS?" —COUNTESS LUANN TO KELLY "YOU AND I ARE EXACTLY THE SAME. YOU'RE BRUNETTE, AND I'M BLONDE. WE'RE VERY VERY SIMILAR." —KELLY "YOU'RE BLONDE?" —BETHENNY "YOU'RE GOING TO SIT THERE WITH YOUR CRAZY EYES AND TELL ME WHO I AM?" —COUNTESS LUANN TO RAMONA "WHERE DO YOU THINK BROOKLYN IS? OHIO?" —JILL "I DON'T WANT TO EAT IN BROOKLYN, OKAY?" —RAMONA

SEASON 3

CAST MEMBERS

JILL ZARIN / KELLY BENSIMON / LUANN DE LESSEPS / SONJA MORGAN / ALEX MCCORD / RAMONA SINGER / BETHENNY FRANKEL

JILL'S HAIR was huge and there was a sticker from SAKS on the bottom of her shoe for much of the reunion.

This was a huge reunion because Bethenny and Jill had fought all season. Bethenny (pregnant and in love) was on her way out the door to shoot her spin-off, *Bethenny Ever After,* and I think that there was a fair amount of resentment from the other women that she was getting her own show. The tension between Bethenny and Jill

"NO WAY YOU GET WHAT SHE'S SAYING. NO ONE IN THE WORLD ON PLANET EARTH GETS WHAT SHE'S SAYING." —BETHENNY TO ANDY, ABOUT KELLY

AIRED

2010

The ladies BROKE the fourth wall a lot at this reunion in discussing who they would and would not FILM with.

that day was through the roof, and they were on either side of me, so that in turn made me incredibly uneasy. I also remember Kelly not being able to land the plane. It was also Sonja's first reunion, and if you watch it today, she is so demure and not much like the Sonja she evolved into.

SEASON 4

CAST MEMBERS

RAMONA SINGER / SONJA MORGAN / ALEX MCCORD / CINDY BARSHOP / KELLY BENSIMON / JILL ZARIN / LUANN DE LESSEPS

My parents came to visit for this reunion and marveled at how loud the women were, and at my inability to do anything about it. This was the first time I had to truly raise my voice. I screamed, "Shut the fuck up!" and it remains a moment I don't love. I do not like

"MAYBE BECAUSE JILL HAS ENOUGH DIRT ON YOU FOR A LANDFILL, YOU HAVE TO BE HER BFF." —ALEX TO COUNTESS LUANN

AIRED

2011

having to scream at women!! We had a feeling going into that reunion that we needed to make major changes to the show, and afterward, we were absolutely committed to a shift.

SEASON 5

CAST MEMBERS

RAMONA SINGER / SONJA MORGAN / LUANN DE LESSEPS / HEATHER THOMSON / CAROLE RADZIWILL / AVIVA DRESCHER

The addition of Carole, Aviva, and Heather took us in entirely new directions, like the Berkshires (although not yet to Blue Stone Manor!). The Countess versus Princess narrative tickled me to no end.

AIRED

2012

SEASON 6

CAST MEMBERS

RAMONA SINGER / SONJA MORGAN / AVIVA DRESCHER / LUANN DE LESSEPS / CAROLE RADZIWILL / HEATHER THOMSON / KRISTEN TAEKMAN

The season ended with Aviva tossing her leg at Le Cirque, and the reunion picked up with hours of absurd banter. Ramona, who was going through her breakup with Mario, was especially furious at my line of questioning, and unsuccessfully tried to turn the tables on me when she demanded, "Well, what about your personal life? Who are

"A HOMELESS GIRL IN IRELAND IS TWEETING FOR YOU?"—ANDY TO SONJA

AIRED

2014

you sleeping with?" I felt that was ridiculous because I hadn't committed to being on a reality show about my personal life, and she agreed to be on one, with her husband, displaying their personal lives. During those years of her breakup, she was so sensitive and hurt and I think she really didn't want to air too much of it out of respect for her daughter. As a parent, I understand.

SEASON 7

CAST MEMBERS

RAMONA SINGER / LUANN DE LESSEPS / DORINDA MEDLEY / SONJA MORGAN / KRISTEN TAEKMAN / HEATHER THOMSON / CAROLE RADZIWILL / BETHENNY FRANKEL

This was the year RAMONA fell ASLEEP, something Mary M. Cosby of *RHOSLC* would do years later.

BETHENNY was back and lit a fire in the room.

AIRED

2015

SEASON 8

CAST MEMBERS

BETHENNY FRANKEL / SONJA MORGAN / CAROLE RADZIWILL / JULES WAINSTEIN / SONJA MORGAN / DORINDA MEDLEY / LUANN DE LESSEPS

Dorinda has entered the chat and came out swinging at this reunion. One thing I will say about Dorinda: She's like Dan Rather. She has a quote for every occasion, and it's always spot-on.

AIRED

2016

SEASON 9

CAST MEMBERS

RAMONA SINGER / SONJA MORGAN / DORINDA MEDLEY / LUANN DE LESSEPS / TINSLEY MORTIMER / CAROLE RADZIWILL / BETHENNY FRANKEL

There was a lot of mystery surrounding Tinsley's love life, Luann's engagement, and Sonja's entire universe that made for an incredibly entertaining day of banter.

AIRED

2017

SEASON 10

CAST MEMBERS

BETHENNY FRANKEL / SONJA MORGAN / RAMONA SINGER / TINSLEY MORTIMER / DORINDA MEDLEY / CAROLE RADZIWILL / LUANN DE LESSEPS (NOT PICTURED)

"YOU'RE NOT AN EXPERT IN BALONEY." —DORINDA TO BETHENNY, WHO CRITICIZED SONJA'S BUSINESS VENTURES

This was the year that Bethenny and Carole's friendship dissolved and so did my friendship with Carole. She and I had known each other for many years before I asked her to join the show. People think that I was firmly on Bethenny's side and I would like to tell you that I wasn't. I remember Carole telling me that I was full of shit AND that I was scared of Bethenny. I wasn't scared of Bethenny, but their

"IF YOU FOUND OUT HE HAD CHEATED ON YOU, WHAT WOULD YOU DO?"—ANDY

"I WOULD DEFINITELY LEAVE."— LUANN

"I'D KILL HIM." —DORINDA

AIRED

2018

breakup was so confusing, frankly, and Carole was so in the weeds about it that as the night went on, I became exhausted by the topic. I kept trying to calm the fight down but it just didn't work. If I rewatched it now, I would probably have some revisionist opinions about that feud. I'm happy to report that after not speaking to each other for many years after this reunion, Carole and I made up and are pals again.

SEASON 11

CAST MEMBERS

LUANN DE LESSEPS / TINSLEY MORTIMER / RAMONA SINGER / SONJA MORGAN / DORINDA MEDLEY / BETHENNY FRANKEL

Factors at play here: Dorinda and Luann were in a weird place; Luann was emerging as a cabaret star; and Ramona was embracing her single life.

I LOVE BETHENNY'S OUTFIT!

AIRED

2019

SEASON 12

CAST MEMBERS

LEAH MCSWEENEY / DORINDA MEDLEY / RAMONA SINGER / LUANN DE LESSEPS / SONJA MORGAN

This COVID year was very weird. We were very happy to be doing an in-person reunion. It was Leah's first season and she had a great one. They all look like a million bucks. Though, after this reunion, Dorinda was put "on pause."

AIRED

2020

SEASON 14

CAST MEMBERS

ERIN LICHY / JENNA LYONS /
SAI DE SILVA / UBAH HASSAN /
BRYNN WHITFIELD / JESSEL TAANK

I still think she's the only housewife to wear JEANS at a reunion.

"DID YOU WATCH THE SHOW, ERIN?" —JESSEL

"I DID." —ERIN

"DO YOU WATCH IT WITH A FUCKING BLINDFOLD OVER YOUR FACE?" —JESSEL

This was our rebooted group featuring Jenna Lyons, who changed the game for reunion outfits two years in a row. It was just such a perfect look: a tux jacket, nothing under it, jeans, and diamonds. I mean, that is iconic!

AIRED

2023

"YOU PUT PEOPLE IN THE HOSPITAL. I PUT PEOPLE IN THE FUNERAL HOME."—BRYNN TO UBAH

SEASON 15

CAST MEMBERS

UBAH HASSAN / ERIN LICHY / SAI DE SILVA / RACQUEL CHEVREMONT / JESSEL TAANK / JENNA LYONS / BRYNN WHITFIELD

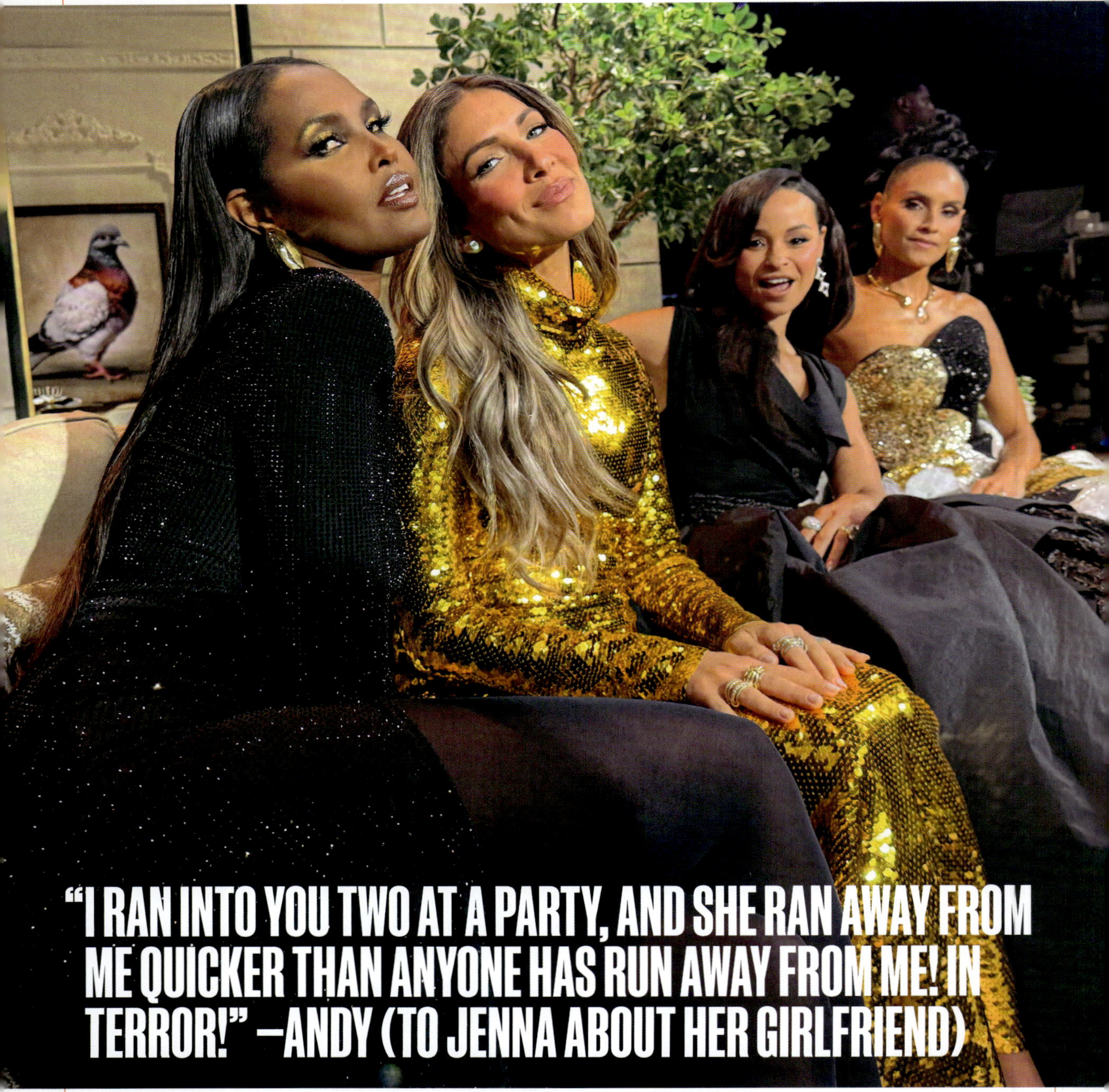

"I RAN INTO YOU TWO AT A PARTY, AND SHE RAN AWAY FROM ME QUICKER THAN ANYONE HAS RUN AWAY FROM ME! IN TERROR!" —ANDY (TO JENNA ABOUT HER GIRLFRIEND)

I loved what the women wore this year! Jenna wearing a robe was a really fun serve. I remember telling her, "You know, you have to take the sunglasses off when we start taping." And she was like, "I do?" Viewers need to see your eyes! Unfortunately, this reunion became incredibly dark, given how the season ended.

AIRED

2025

OTHER REUNIONS

I love hosting the reunions for non-*Housewives* shows because I feel like I can get more in the dirt. I can be a little more opinionated because I'm not a producer of those shows (although I was in the early years, but I left to do *Watch What Happens Live* and *The Real Housewives* full-time). Shows like *Vanderpump Rules, Summer House,* and *Southern Charm* have been built around caddish behavior by Peter Pan–type guys, and I especially love giving them shit and calling them out on their behavior. Maybe it's easier for me to give men the business because I am one, but I love to let it rip on these guys. I am including the *Housewives* franchises that are no longer on the air in this section, too. (And, yes, I get a little sad thinking of what might have been when I look at those pics in particular. The women work so hard to give their all to the show, and I wanna reach through the pics and give them a hug or high five, their choice.)

VANDERPUMP RULES

I love doing *Vanderpump Rules* reunions. Lisa and I share a special relationship. We always begin the filming day with a kiki in her dressing room where she gives me the most up-to-date gossip about what's going on with the SUR-vers.

I had forgotten that we brought Stassi's younger brother out to insult the rest of the cast, which did not go over well with most of them.

When I look at the early *Vanderpump Rules* reunions, I'm really struck by how young and beautiful they all are. I remember Tom Sandoval always looked like an anime character to me and I was always struck by his willingness to just let his emotions overtake him, sometimes to the point of tears, which I always admire in a man.

"I'VE NEVER HAD A GIRL SAY NO TO ME BEFORE." –JAX TAYLOR

The most stressful of all the *Vanderpump* reunions was, of course, the year of Scandoval. I didn't think we would get through the day of filming with the three principals involved remaining in the room; I thought that one of them was going to bolt. And because of that, and because we wanted each of them to have their say, I did three separate interviews with Tom, Ariana, and Raquel the day before the reunion, so that their perspectives and stories would be told very clearly. We didn't wind up having to use those as much because we got it all in the room. I will never forget the moment Ariana walked out in that dress. Someone who had been part of the ensemble really emerged as an individual force to be reckoned with. That show turned out to be an important part of Bravo history.

SHAHS OF SUNSET

I always had mixed feelings about *Shahs of Sunset* reunions because in that setting the group, each of whom I liked very much individually, came together nastier and more cutthroat than any other ensemble cast on Bravo—past, present, or future. They went for blood every time, and each reunion was dark in some way (with the exception of one where we were all sitting at a table with a lavish spread of incredible Persian food).

"WHEN MJ IS THE VOICE OF REASON, YOU KNOW WE'RE IN BIG TROUBLE." —REZA FARAHAN

MARRIED TO MEDICINE

I love hosting *Married to Medicine* reunions. The ladies are so smart and insightful, and they generally really care about one another. Year after year I come away learning something about what it is to be a person of color in their industry. It always tickles me having Simone and Jackie on either side of me, and I joke every year about how loud Simone is in my right ear. And every year, her decibels remain intact. The season where we saved Dr. Simone's marriage in the room remains to this day one of the best reunions I've been a part of on Bravo.

SOUTHERN CHARM

The drama changes every year on *Southern Charm*, but the people remain very much who they are. I love that they are so specific to where they live. After all these years, Austen, Shep, and Craig still crack me up, and they're so easy to rib!

"WHY DO YOU WANT TO SEE CRAIG'S DICK?"—ANDY, TO AUSTEN

"IT'S WEIRD, I'VE KNOWN YOU FOR TOO LONG, I HAVEN'T SEEN YOUR DICK! MAYBE I AM IN LOVE WITH CRAIG."—AUSTEN

SUMMER HOUSE

In the early seasons of *Summer House*, I was not especially fond of hosting their (Clubhouse) reunions. The show had not yet caught wind, but Bravo was committed to making it work. Boy, am I glad, because by season four it was off to the races.

In season ten, the fellas wound up getting burgers around the corner from my house and I popped over and joined them for a drink, a rare occurrence (meeting up with cast members, not having a drink after a reunion).

This was the most anticipated *Summer House* reunion in the show's history and brought it into the zeitgeist in a way it wasn't before. It was also the most emotional I had ever seen the cast. The carnage from the West-Amanda affair created a tearful and sad end to what had been the most fun season in the show's run. Also, by the end of the night, audio from the taping leaked and caused a viral frenzy.

THE REAL HOUSEWIVES OF D.C.

Other than the reunions where I had to grill Erika Jayne about her legal woes or Scandoval, I prepared the hardest for the *D.C.* reunion, knowing how many eyeballs there would be on a single interview. There's something about the FBI asking for your raw tapes because one of your cast members crashed a state dinner that makes it clear that the show will probably not return. That being said, I loved *The Real Housewives of D.C.* and was very upset that we couldn't pick it up for a second season. It was racially diverse, it touched on politics, and, in essence, it was a show about

living in proximity to power and the lengths people go to get there. Interviewing Michaele Salahi was a very circular affair. I asked if she had really been a Redskins cheerleader and if she had also been invited to the White House (on the list or none of the above). The other women believed none of what she had to say. I left the day feeling sympathetic toward her. Go have a rewatch of that season and reunion. It deserves your attention.

THE REAL HOUSEWIVES OF DUBAI

The Dubai *Housewives* just screams excess, much like the city they're from. As much as I loved that Ayan and Stanbury squashed their sizable beef for season two, I—and the viewers—were very upset that no one in the group could find peace at the reunion. Had they been able to, I think the show might have gotten another chance. But there was no turning back. Some housewives mistakenly think that conflict is going to keep them on the show and keep the show going, but in truth, drama has an expiration date.

THE REAL HOUSEWIVES OF DALLAS

When the *Dallas* housewives were good, they were great. LeeAnne Locken provided some iconic *Housewives* moments. I loved watching D'Andra and her mother, and Stephanie's friendship with Brandi warmed my heart. I initially didn't know what to make of Kameron Westcott! When she joined the show, I really thought she was putting on an act, but it turns out she is exactly who she is.

ANDY'S BABY SHOWER

When I announced on *WWHL* that I was having a baby, I did it in front of a group of stunned OGs who, the second the show went off the air, surrounded me in the most loving, nurturing way and immediately declared they were going to throw me a joint baby shower. I was blown away by their kindness and maternal instincts, which were focused like a laser on me. The date was set for two weeks before Ben's due date at the Palm Restaurant in Beverly Hills. Every single current housewife from every franchise currently on air was invited, and most came. This was before BravoCon and was the first time an event of this scope had happened. There were no cameras except on our phones and that of Bravo's Charles Sykes, whose work appears throughout these next pages. The energy was through the roof and it's safe to say there hasn't been a baby shower like it since.

The event would not have happened without my best friend, Bruce, who lent us the Palm and got a kick out of working hand in hand with Kyle on the planning of the shower.

I love this picture of me and the hosts for the event. I had it printed out and framed as a thank-you gift for each of the ladies a month later. I especially have to give Kyle her flowers because I got the sense she did most of the real legwork for the event, even though all the ladies threw it for me.

This group photo is one for the ages. To anyone with taste, it's like the Avengers. It's funny to see who showed up that day and who didn't and who's still in the fold and who isn't. Definitely a moment in time.

Imagine my joy when John Mayer said he wanted to attend. I kept explaining to him who would be there and what would happen, and he kept saying, "I need to meet your work friends." Oh, here are Nene and Vicki explaining to John the ins and outs of being a housewife.

Each of the women made a toast and I can't fully express how moved I was. I felt so much love from them. You can listen to it on Radio Andy. (We didn't shoot the event for TV, but I had mics there recording a special for the radio.)

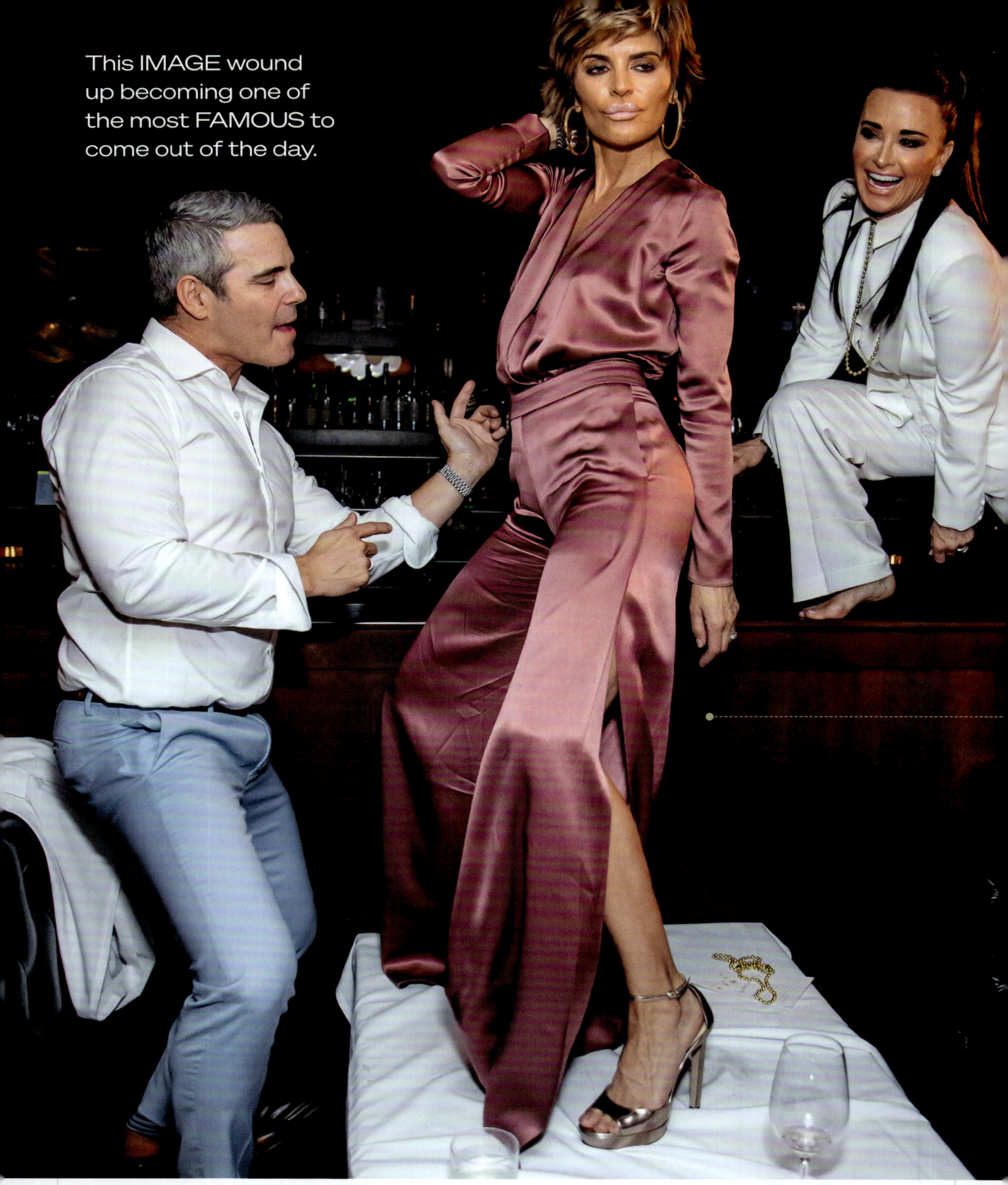

This IMAGE wound up becoming one of the most FAMOUS to come out of the day.

Lisa Rinna gets the MVP for the day. She famously encouraged all the housewives to get up on the table and dance for me. I now view her as the ultimate hype person, and I think she could open a church.

Look at this incredible table. Not-so-fun fact: There weren't enough seats for everybody, so Emily Simpson and Gina Kirschenheiter had to sit at a nearby booth, which seemed like a kids' table. I felt terrible.

HOUSEWIVES WITH ANDY'S FAMILY

Phaedra and Porsha got a huge kick out of my mom at the *Watch What Happens Live* fifteenth-anniversary party.

My dad is a charmer, but the big flirtation that night was between my mom and Joe Gorga.

Ben thought that Phaedra and Porsha were superheroes that day and he wasn't wrong.

This is one of the funniest pictures. My daughter, Lucy, does not seem to be buying what Luann is selling.

I brought Ben by Vicki's hotel room to meet the OG of the *OC* and she smothered him with "woo hoos."

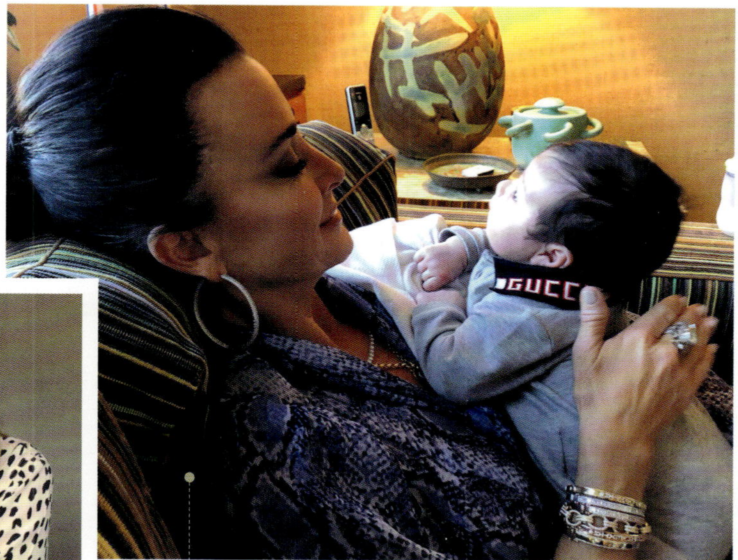

Kyle was so sweet about everything relating to the birth of my children and came to see Ben a few weeks after he was born. I believe that the Gucci onesie Ben is wearing was from Karen Huger.

My mom always got a kick out of Nene, and I got a kick out of their height difference.

Here's Ben at Luann's house in Sag Harbor. I love seeing the motherly side of the housewives through the lens of my kids.

BRAVOCON

The day officially begins when you first set foot on the pavement and are greeted by screaming Bravo fans outside. It's tremendous for the ego! Then again, BravoCon was made to feed the fans and all our egos.

There's a huge "backstage" area at BravoCon with passageways that get you to the events. You run into every combination of Bravolebrity in those halls. And here I am with the talls, and Kyle and I are the smalls.

Greeting Bozoma Saint John. This was her first BravoCon.

Why wouldn't I run into Gia Giudice and Kiki Barth together?

Taking a SELFIE with Mr. Dimples, Craig Conover.

I believe this was the moment Captain Jason told me he was not drinking all weekend. Look at my shocked response.

This was the first time I'd seen Teddi Mellencamp since her health battle, and we had a real moment on the blue carpet. Yes, that's Kyle looking on.

Over the years, Scheana Shay and I have taken hundreds of selfies. She has a specific pose!!

Welcoming Rachel Zoe back into the Bravo fold as she welcomes me into a forest of fake fur.

Giving my best SMIZE.

Walking to my panel, arm in arm with Jeff Lewis. Little did I know that I would be furious with him ten minutes later. I'd rather not restart an argument, but the headline is: I felt this interview was all too negative.

Here are Jeff and I on the BravoCon stage.

Rehearsing for The Bravos. The cardboard posters, each signifying where the Bravolebrities would be sitting. To me, a better crowd with bigger stars than the Oscars!

Stopping by Meredith Marks's DJ set.

Having a serious moment with *Watch What Happens Live* executive producer Deirdre Connolly, the GOAT of late-night producers.

Rehearsing for my musical number, and I can guarantee I did so much better during rehearsals than I did on the show. I am not a singer! And so far, I'm two for two with nerves getting the best of me.

FaceTiming with Ben and Lucy.

Looking at the cardboard posters with *Bitch Sesh*'s Casey Wilson.

Doing a mock walk-through in the audience.

I've been around a galaxy of housewives who can't sing, and now they've been around a host who can't either. At least I tried.

My talent producer Carly Liotta took this picture of me and Vicki backstage holding hands, having a very deep conversation. Little did Vicki know that I had an orange in my back pocket that was about to change her life.

My highlight of BravoCon 2025 was giving Vicki back her orange.

SALT LAKE CITY housewives were the biggest stars of the weekend.

With Shereé, Phaedra, and Larsa. I think Shereé put this huge smile on my face, but also, I have never been happier than I was in that suit.

Everyone's so TALL. I'm 5' 9".

With Jerry O'Connell and Lindsay and Austen moments after Lindsay informed the group she was ovulating and I instructed Austen to wear a condom.

With a fedora, Luann was the hit of the party.

This is at The Bravos after-party. Vicki carried her orange around all weekend long.

With Adriana, who still had her envelope; she won the "Who Said That?" Award for Colloquial Excellence for her Haitian mortician line.

Arm in arm with Craig.

Checking in with Jesse about how he felt when I ribbed him and Erika Jayne. He took it like a champ.

With the basketball wives, Larsa and Angela.

PAST BRAVOCONS

Backstage at BravoCon. It's as chaotic and magical as you would hope.

This is Chanel Ayan in an understated Flying-Nun-meets-Met-Gala ensemble.

Here I am with a mini–*Orange County* reunion after giving Vicki Gunvalson her Wifetime Achievement Award.

I will never tire of backstage party pics, mixing folks together from shows! Where else would we get Kyle Cooke, Paige DeSorbo, Amanda Batula, and Craig Conover hanging out with the Grande Dame?

I love this picture of Nene mugging backstage at a shoot in 2019. Doesn't she look beautiful?

Squashing the beef in 2023 with Vicki and Dorinda.

Singing "Tardy for the Party" with Kim Zolciak was a true honor.

I believe Kenya ate Vicki for lunch in this beef squash.

At the Legends Ball with two legends at the 2022 BravoCon.

Me ARRIVING and SURPRISING the women.

The folks at Bravo decided that the best way to celebrate twenty years of such an iconic franchise would be to bring back *Ultimate Girls Trip* with the core cast visiting *Housewives* cities (Orange County, Beverly Hills, Atlanta, Miami, and New York) culminating with a big finale party at Dorinda's Blue Stone Manor in the Berkshires, which, of course, was the site of many memorable *Housewives* moments. I was thrilled when production asked if I would consider surprising the women at that party! No one knew about the surprise, except somehow Shereé, who mentioned it to me on the phone a week before the Berkshires. I made her swear that she wouldn't tell anyone. Shereé isn't called the bone collector for nothing!

On the drive up, I wrote a toast celebrating the women. I'm not a person who is ever nervous speaking publicly; it's what I do for a living, I've been on live television around the world without breaking a sweat. But I have to say, standing there in front of these women who have meant so much to me, my hands were "shaking, physically shaking" (to quote Lisa Barlow). It was a measure of how impactful these women were and how important it was for me to get this toast right. Walking in and surprising them was so surreal. Shockingly, I had never been to Blue Stone Manor after all these years, and so that in and of itself was like stepping into my absolute favorite TV show. It

was so overwhelming, looking around the room and seeing nothing but housewives, like my baby shower only way more intense because there were cameras. We were at Blue Stone Manor, and we were all dressed to the nines in our *Gilded Age* drag.

I was only there for two hours, partly because I think production didn't want me there for the whole night, but also because I had to relieve a babysitter back in the city (who had a rave to go to at midnight). I was hosting Ben's seventh birthday party the next morning, too, or I would have stayed all night. The mood was electric! It was so happy and super celebratory and emotional.

It was the truest form of sisterhood that I had seen among the ladies. I did try to broker peace between Lisa Barlow and Heather Gay, and it went terribly wrong and resulted in a pretty large-scale verbal altercation. Along the road trip, Lisa Barlow had made allies out of Kyle, Porsha, and the rest of her castmates, who were all kind of joining her team, and Heather didn't feel good about any of this. I in turn felt terrible for lighting the match.

Another match I lit was between Melissa and Teresa, but that one had a more positive outcome. I brought up the root of their issue, which is how Melissa joined the show, and both Melissa and I were able to say some things that made Teresa happy. It was an absolutely euphoric night.

Pulling Melissa and Teresa aside for a chat. I actually had fun doing this, not at a reunion and actually at the Berkshires.

The Atlanta gals arrived fashionably late, due to, as they reported to me, their luggage being lost. I said, I know exactly when it will be back: "Spring / summer, September." We howled. I love them.

I spent a good twenty minutes in Dorinda's historic dining room chatting with the ladies, and when Alex McCord walked in, I demanded they all give her a big round of applause. That was the vibe for the entire night.

The Real Housewives of Rhode Island officially became "Housewives" that night when they met me for the first time, plus superstars from across the *Housewives* universe. That didn't stop them from getting into it in Dorinda's living room. What is it about Blue Stone Manor . . .

Toward the end of the night, Luann put Vicki on a throne for a toast, and I somehow got pulled into it. It was wonderful to see the OG of the OC get her due.

Here I am making my WOBBLY TOAST. I was especially EMOTIONAL, looking into the women's eyes as I did it.

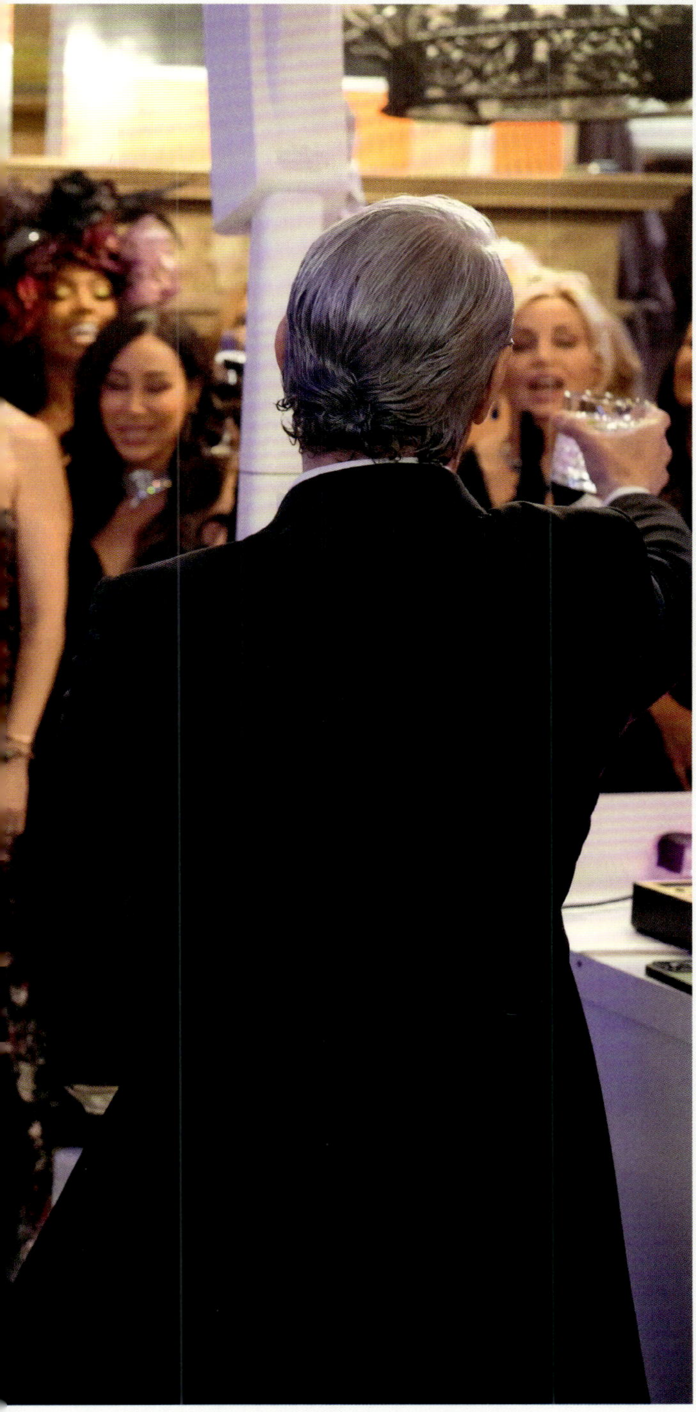

ANDY'S TOAST

There are 175 million women in America, so there are arguably 175 million women who might refer to themselves at one point or another as a real housewife. But there have been just under two hundred of YOU—THE *Real Housewives*. You were amazing women before we ever met you, and now you are each exceptional . . . superstars known worldwide. Worldwide! For twenty years YOU have dominated pop culture. People don't understand how hard it is to be you and do what you do. You share your life with us. . . . You serve yourselves up for the judgment of millions of strangers. You make us laugh and cry and mad and sad and cheer from our living rooms. Man, do you entertain us. You get in hair and makeup when you don't want to. You host incredible events and vacations. You figure out what to wear to lunch and dinner and shopping and a walk and *Great Gatsby* parties and every damn place you go. You speak your feelings and hear the sometimes bitter truth of what others think of you. You deal with the pettiest fucking bullshit. We see you at your best and your worst. You are strong and vulnerable all at once. Most of all—you are yourselves. And you are each proof that being yourself is all you ever need to be. Ladies—you are my Avengers. And ladies—for twenty years—you have meant the world to me. THANK YOU. Here's to you. Here's to the real housewives.

ACKNOWLEDGMENTS

Thanks to everyone at Penguin Random House for their enthusiasm and energy surrounding this labor of love—especially my partner in all great books, Gillian Blake. Thanks to Lori Kusatzky for her guidance and institutional knowledge of the most important things in life, namely Bravo. Thank you to my researcher (and Bravo savant), Lukas Thimm, who rewatched countless hours of reunions and mined thousands of personal photos to get this book absolutely right. Thank you to the brilliant Laura Palese for bringing this book to life vibrantly and with love.

ABOUT THE AUTHOR

Andy Cohen is the author of five *New York Times* bestselling books. He is the host and executive producer of *Watch What Happens Live*, Bravo's late-night interactive talk show. He also serves as executive producer of the *Real Housewives* franchise and hosts the network's highly rated reunion specials. He's won an Emmy and five Peabody Awards for his work, and he lives in New York City with his two children.